Festival Elephants
and the
Myth of Global Poverty

Festival Elephants
and the
Myth of Global Poverty

Glynn Cochrane

Boston   New York   San Francisco

Mexico City   Montreal   Toronto   London   Madrid   Munich   Paris

Hong Kong   Singapore   Tokyo   Cape Town   Sydney

Senior Series Editor: *Dave Repetto*
Series Editorial Assistant: *Jack Cashman*
Marketing Manager: *Laura Lee Manley*
Production Editor: *Pat Torelli*
Editorial Production Service: *Nesbitt Graphics, Inc.*
Composition Buyer: *Linda Cox*
Manufacturing Buyer: *Debbie Rossi*
Electronic Composition: *Nesbitt Graphics, Inc.*
Interior Design: *Nesbitt Graphics, Inc.*
Cover Administrator: *Kristina Mose-Libon*
Cover Designer: *Bernadette Skok*

For related titles and support materials, visit our online catalog at
www.ablongman.com.

Between the time website information is gathered and then published, it is
not unusual for some sites to have closed. Also, the transcription of URLs
can result in typographical errors. The publisher would appreciate
notification where these errors occur so that they may be corrected in
subsequent editions.

ISBN-13: 978-0-205-57765-1   ISBN-10: 0-205-57765-2

Library of Congress Cataloging-in-Publication Data

Cochrane, Glynn.
  Festival elephants and the myth of global poverty / by Glynn Cochrane.
     p. cm.
  Includes bibliographical references.
  ISBN 0-205-57765-2
  1. Economic assistance–Developing countries. 2. Poverty–Developing
countries. 3. International agencies–Developing countries–Sociological
aspects. I. Title.

HC60.C544 2008
339.4'6091724–dc22
                        2007046437

Printed in the United States of America

10   9   8   7   6   5   4   3   2   1   12   11   10   09   08

Dedication

"Je me retire pour mieux resortir."
d'après Talleyrand, évoqué par Judith

Contents

Preface

This book contains accounts of my personal experiences with aid agency operations in poor countries, their various successes and failures, their paradoxes, their harmonies and their dissonances. When I started working as an administrator in the tropics in 1962, the British Ministry of Overseas Development placed great emphasis on staff having in-country experience, cultural competence, and grassroots skills. You would not expect to rise to a policy-making role unless you had had significant local experience in a developing country. In those days, global aid agencies had ground staff who were genuinely knowledgeable about local conditions among the poor, and so they were able to offer sensible advice to both governments and aid agencies.

Since the 1980s, I have noticed a fundamental shift as global aid agencies developed ever-more ambitious plans to tackle what I call the "Myth of Global Poverty." Misguided by the Myth, global aid agencies and civil society organizations are also hobbled by the lack of staff with hands-on skills and grassroots experience. A seemingly positive trend, to hire more country-resident staff, does not fill the gap because these people tend to live in the capital cities and become another cog in the central bureaucracy. Like the staff at agency headquarters, they fail to understand the local nuances of poverty and therefore fail to contribute to a solution.

In this book you will meet individuals I refer to as "Festival Elephants." Prompted by the global ambitions of their agencies, they grandstand in poor countries and make eye-catching promises to put on a good show. Although their job is to end poverty, poverty is thriving. Is it the Festival Elephant's fault that he or she can do little more than dance and prance? No. I do not assign culpability to any individual. Instead, I point to underlying causes within the aid business, including its current philosophy (the Myth of Global Poverty) and the misalignment of staff skills in relation to publicly stated goals.

In the final two chapters, I make suggestions for change, which center around the need to bring back what I call Worker Elephants. Worker Elephants are not flashy, they do not avoid getting muddy if their task requires it, and they accomplish tasks one-by-one. You will read how pleased I was to reconnect with many Worker Elephants in the mining industry.

According to accepted ethical guidelines in anthropology, I do not name or otherwise identify particular Elephants in this book. Any resemblance to real individuals is, especially in the fictionalized vignettes, unintended. The views expressed in this book are mine alone and should not be attributed to any of the institutions, such as the UNDP or the World Bank or organizations such as Rio Tinto, for which I have worked.

Thanks to Kate Schindler and Claire Twomey, Program Assistants of the Culture in Global Affairs Research and Policy Program and BA graduates in International Affairs at George Washington University, for bibliographic and other research.

Glynn Cochrane
Edinburgh, Scotland

About the Author

Glynn Cochrane started his career as a District Officer and then District Commissioner in the British Overseas Civil Service working with villagers in the Solomon Islands. After doing a D.Phil. in Social Anthropology at Oxford and writing *Big Men and Cargo Cults*, he was professor of anthropology and department chair at Syracuse University. In the 1970s, he was invited to advise the World Bank on the use of anthropology in their operations. Later he developed and wrote *Social Soundness Analysis* for the U.S. Agency for International Development, a social appraisal system for projects that has been used by the agency for over thirty years. His books, *Development Anthropology* and *The Cultural Appraisal of Development Projects*, captured some of these experiences. In the 1980s, he became Director of USAID's worldwide Co-operative Agreement between the agency and Syracuse University, the Local Revenue Administration Project (LRAP) that was headquartered at Syracuse. During a sabbatical year spent at the World Bank in 1983, he wrote *Policies for Strengthening Third World Local Government* for the 1983 *World Development Report*.

His overseas experience includes, in addition to time spent in the Solomon islands, long-term assignments in the Cook Islands, Tanzania, Papua New Guinea, and Sri Lanka undertaken for the World Bank, UNDP, and USAID. In 1995, he began to work with the mining company Rio Tinto plc as the company's advisor on social issues responsible for assisting with the development of policies and procedures related to community relations in more than sixty operations in twenty-six countries around the world.

Festival Elephants
and the
Myth of Global Poverty

1

〰

The Myth of Global Poverty

Since the 1970s, the budgets and influence of global aid agencies and global civil society organizations have grown enormously because of their invention and patenting of the idea that there is such a thing as global poverty, and that they have the skills to cure it.

The invention of global poverty, and global fixes for it, occurred during Robert McNamara's tenure as President of the World Bank in the late 1960s and early 1970s. McNamara, who served as the U.S. Secretary of Defense during the Vietnam War, was noted for believing that a problem that had not been quantified was a problem that had not been properly thought-through. Along these lines, McNamara's staff concluded that poverty could be seen as a homogeneous category for which objective, quantifiable, cash income/material consumption standards could be defined and measured. In effect, the World Bank homogenized the milk of human kindness.

Each global aid agency, conscious of the budgetary advantages that go with being seen to do something important about poverty, claims that it plays a critical role in the campaign against global poverty. Such UN agencies as the United Nations Environment Programme, the United Nations Development Programme, UNICEF, and UNESCO all regularly make bids to help the poor. The UN High Commission for Human Rights says that poverty is an infringement of human rights. The World Bank says that only with its development skills and its comprehensive development framework can the systemic problems that cause poverty be addressed.

UN agencies appeal to the public for funds. On overseas commercial flights, passengers are asked to give money to help UNICEF. The morning news on the radio, television, or Internet carries stories about how the World Bank is going to help poor people in Macedonia, or Palestine, or some other newsworthy part of the world. Such features do not mention the very high costs of UN poverty assistance. It can cost hundreds of thousands of dollars a year to keep a UN staff member in a poor country. And that applies to UNICEF staff as well.

Using the McNamara approach, global aid agencies were able to develop global programs to take care of every problem known to poor people everywhere in order to make poverty history. If people all over the world lack clean water or medicine, give them more money; if they are illiterate, give them more money; if they are malnourished, give them more money; if they are ill-served by their government, give them more money. No one bothers to ask the poor about what they want or if they approve of what the global aid agencies propose.

During the later 1970s, when the Myth of Global Poverty (hereafter referred to as "the Myth") was being constructed and popularized among development aid institutions, few people in the large aid agencies paid attention to the cultural context of poverty, or to what the poor thought or how they really lived. They did not spend time with the communities whose interests they supposedly represented. The same is true of the growing number of large civil society organizations, such as CARE and Oxfam. According to the Myth, the entire way of life of the poor would be eliminated using money, the weapon of mass development. Cultural knowledge and sustained interaction with poor people were not in the arsenal for the War on Poverty.

The logic of the Myth works like this: Poverty is defined as global, that is, the same everywhere. The answer to global poverty then is to provide more aid, through loans and grants, to governments of poor countries. The global aid institutions, therefore, need more and more money. To raise more money to lend, the agencies speak on behalf of the world's poor, as if they were ventriloquists for them. They turned into publishing houses that specialize in detailing the suffering of the poor, spewing out more and more statistical material detailing the suffering of the global poor. When aid agencies put out so much information about what the poor do not have, and so little on what they do have, they render the poor inhuman, unrecognizable as individuals. Removed from their social contexts and transformed by negative assumptions and benumbing statistics, the poor become wards of aid agencies and civil society organizations. Because the agencies' vision of poverty lacks a human face, it therefore does not require personal relationships with the poor, or hands-on skills for learning about the poor.

For the three decades since the 1970s, the Myth has deceived global aid agencies and civil society organizations leaders into promising, but not delivering benefits that seem so obvious that only corrupt, incompetent, or lazy leadership in the poor countries would fail to ensure implementation.

The Myth does not recognize that poor people everywhere, from Tijuana to Tahiti, are poor for different reasons and experience poverty in different ways. These differences are not sufficiently understood and accommodated by the global organizations offering assistance, and so what can be accomplished by development assistance is greatly overestimated. Global aid agencies fail to alleviate poverty because more and more international development assistance personnel have no direct experience of the real life of poor people. To them, poor people are little more than a "target." They overlook the fact that poor people have ideas, knowledge, and aspirations; that they wish to be treated with respect and as potential partners in any plans for them. The result is that the aid agencies are much better at raising their public profile as the main hope for the world's poor than at providing a grassroots demonstration of how to eliminate poverty.

The Myth has constructed an image of billions of faceless and voiceless poor people. Such poor people do not exist. They are a statistical artifact. At the same time, the Myth suggests that it is not important to know about local people and their lives, and about how poverty is experienced in particular social contexts by real people. Aid agencies, freed from learning about the aspirations and abilities of the poor, have concentrated on what the poor did not have in a material sense. They could then showcase their own abilities to supply materialistic solutions that matched the results provided by aggregated statistical analyses.

The Myth treats cultural factors as extrinsic variables, something that can be added in after all the important decisions had been taken. But cultural factors are intrinsic to the local scene: They are not the paint or the backdrop, but the bricks and mortar. To an anthropologist, whose job is to know real people and how they live in particular contexts, cultural factors make all the difference.

A program to eliminate so-called global poverty makes as much sense as a program to eliminate global laughter or a program to persuade everyone to eat rice. Could we have a program to increase or reduce global laughter or to have one world food? Could we expect people all over the world to laugh at the same joke or to want to eat the same food? No, because laughter and food are deeply embedded in culture.

Poverty, of course, is not a myth. Poverty exists in the world and does not seem to be on the decline. But poverty throughout the world does not correspond in any meaningful way to the monolithic, one-size-fits-all concept of global poverty that is popularized by development assistance agencies and civil society organizations in order to raise funds and generate support in the rich countries.

Overlooking the Local and Abandoning the Anthropological Tradition of Fieldwork

The massive centralization of aid for which the Myth is responsible has reversed a long-standing tradition of making community-level assistance the focal point for poverty alleviation. Local government has been neglected by development assistance since the 1970s, even though, given the poverty mandate, strengthening it should have been a priority.

Operating on a local level is not a new concept. In Britain, for example, alleviating poverty has long been seen as having an important local dimension since a 1598 resolution by justices of the peace in the Elizabethan England meeting at Speenhamland. The Old Poor Law of 1601 was based on the idea that poverty relief needed to be related to community action. Elizabethan England wanted the identification of poverty, as well as the organization and delivery of assistance, to occur at a local level. They recognized that it is only at the local level that poverty can be defined by local people and thereby understood by outsiders who wish to help. It is at the local level that personalities and local circumstances can be recognized. It is at the local level that relationships between outsiders and people who live in poverty must be built.

The Myth was constructed from information collected through questionnaires and other short-term data-gathering endeavors designed by office-based professionals working in rich countries. One noteworthy attempt to include the "voices" of the poor in World Bank thinking, *Voices of the Poor: From Many Lands,* reduced the many and varied voices of poor people worldwide to a single, global voice that says, at the same time, everything (about Global Poverty) and nothing (about Local Poverty). This rendering of the local into the global is clear in the words of James Wolfensohn, President of the World Bank Group, in his 1999 address to the Board of Governors of the Bank:

My colleagues and I decided that, in order to map our own course for the future, we needed to know more about our clients as individuals. We launched a study entitled "Voices of the Poor" and spoke to them about their hopes, their aspirations, their realities. Teams from the Bank gathered the voices of 60,000 men and women in 60 countries. Let me share with you our findings.

Poverty is much more than a matter of income alone. The poor seek a sense of well-being which is peace of mind; it is good health, community, and safety. It is choice and freedom as well as a steady source of income . . . when asked what makes the greatest difference in their lives . . . they say, organizations of their own . . .

As we sit here in Washington we must hear their aspirations. For they are no different from our own (1999:3–5).

The Bank's analysis of the voices of many thousands of poor people reduced their locally varied perceptions of well-being and ill-being to five global dimensions: material well being, health, security, freedom of choice and action, and social agency. In a grand rhetorical flourish, Wolfensohn provided an even more cooked down statement, saying that the aspirations of the poor are no different from those of the very highly paid members of the World Bank's Board of Governors. At some ethereal existential level, this statement may be true, but one then must ask about the size of the gap between aspirations and achieving those aspirations for the poor in comparison to "us."

Just like the global aid agencies, global civil society organizations that subscribe to the Myth send questionnaires to businesses with international interests from beer brewing to shoe manufacturing—questionnaires designed in offices in the rich countries. The surveys ask businesses to put a check in a box. This process reduces, simplifies, and standardizes extremely complex and highly varying community situations in order to provide simple and effective talking points for communication with their fundraisers and the public, and a rationale for monitoring international business.

With its reliance on people-distant questionnaires as the primary research method, the Myth turned the clock back 100 years, ignoring anthropology's signature research methods, fieldwork and participant observation, that produce reliable data on local cultural and social variations. In the nineteenth century, early anthropologists wrote books about "savages" on the basis of "armchair reflection" in much the same way that global programs are now developed. Instead of visiting with and talking to the so-called savages, the authors got information from travelers' writings. They sometimes designed questionnaires and sent them to reliable travelers and others in the field, in the hope that, once completed, they would confirm what the armchair anthropologists had thought in the first place. For example, because the Victorians believed that the so-called savages were sexually promiscuous, any salacious details about such matters were believed and repeated, in much the same way that stories today about corruption or waste by poor country governments are accepted as true, without checking the quality of the information. These early anthropologists, just like the top officials in big aid organizations and big civil society organizations know little from firsthand experience about the realities of local culture, its complexity, and variation.

Victorian anthropologists believed, just as staff in the aid agencies and civil society organizations believe, that their way of life represented the apogee of civilization, that they had a duty to explain the misguided life of "savages" to their countrymen at home. They stressed the potential of "savages" for improvement, despite their lack of cleanliness and godliness, in much the same way that publications and television advertisements tell us that if only we give so much a month, we can cut through all the barriers to improvement that exist in poor countries. This logic made the moral case for the "white man's burden" and British imperialism.

Today, those in aid agencies who send questionnaires from the office are convinced that they also represent a way of life that all should aspire to. Implementation does not seem to them to present any special difficulties, provided the advice that is offered is accepted. Like today's aid agency officials, none of the eminent armchair anthropologists thought that it was necessary to go and live with "savages." When asked by a visitor if he had ever met any of the "savages" he had described so convincingly, Sir James Frazer, the early Cambridge social anthropologist, replied, "Good Heavens, no!"

So when, for example, the response to a questionnaire indicated that "savages" thought gold was a cure for jaundice, the armchair anthropologists concluded that the "savages" did not understand the relationship between cause and effect. Nor, they said, did "savages" understand the connection between sexual intercourse and pregnancy because they called several women "Mother." In fact the "savages" had no more problem with cause and effect than we do. If a "savage" fell out of a tree and broke his arm, he had no difficulty understanding that contact with the ground caused the injury. But, like us, he wanted to know "Why me?" and "Why now?" As for the confusion over motherhood, later fieldwork-based kinship studies showed that the mother term was not the result of confusion but simply a term that implied this is a woman of my mother's generation.

Two events persuaded the armchair anthropologists to move out of their armchairs into the field. One was the expedition by Cambridge University to the Torres Straits in 1898; the other was the publication of Bronislaw Malinowski's research during World War I, based on his four years of residence in the Trobriand Islands in New Guinea. These events established the value of fieldwork and participant observation;

the process whereby, in order to understand a particular society, an anthropologist lives with the "savages" for a long period of time, often several years, learning their language and customs. Fieldwork showed that people's behavior had to be understood in the context of the beliefs, values, and attitudes of the society being studied. Malinowski discovered, for example, that sexual propriety for a young South Sea Islander was not the same thing as sexual propriety for an Australian plantation owner in New Guinea.

Thus, armchair anthropology was overturned in favor of detailed, in-person, on-the-ground studies of particular societies. Fieldwork and participant observation became essential for understanding what people do and think; why they do what they do and think what they do; and how they react to change. Now, because of an enduring tradition of armchair-thinking prevalent in aid agencies, aid policy-makers believe they can create economic growth and eliminate global poverty by pouring vast sums of money into the top level of the governments of poor countries. Dispensing money in this kind of top-down way doesn't work; students of development assistance have known since the 1970s that the funds go to help the well-off. If we needed a recent reminder of the limitations of only supplying money, witness the aid organizations' response to the Asian tsunami of 2005. While huge amounts of money were raised in rich countries, because humanitarian aid organizations did not understand the local scene, much of the money was diverted into the bank accounts of the well-off or was simply wasted. Many of the benefits missed the people in need.

In the next chapter, I show how the Myth has been responsible for the decline, from the 1960s and early 1970s, of hands-on community skills and culturally competent programs and policies and the decline of training people in hands-on skills in global development agencies and civil society institutions. Chapter 3 describes my apprenticeship in the Solomon Islands in the 1960s, where I began to learn from and work with the local people. Chapter 4 takes us to Papua New Guinea and the Cook Islands, where I describe the beginning of the takeover of the Myth of Global Poverty. That story continues in Chapter 5, in the context of Tanzania. Chapter 6 reports on my surprising discovery of hands-on community skills in the mining industry. In Chapter 7, I offer some ideas about how to bring back hands-on skills and field-work for more effectively alleviating poverty.

Along the way, I provide vignettes of fictional characters drawn from my encounters, which occurred with sufficient frequency to make these sketches representative. Some of these stories are about people who believe in global approaches, others are about those who believe in local approaches, and others fit in neither category.

Reading

Narayan, Deepa, ed. 2002. Voices of the Poor: From Many Lands. New York: Oxford University Press for the World Bank.

2

Lessons from Elephants
in Sri Lanka

I asked my friend Nimal, who worked for the Janasavia Poverty Foundation in Sri Lanka, what he thought about the possible success of aid agencies in reaching the poor. "Ah," he said, "they have moved on to global poverty. A few years ago they were promising us land for the landless, homes for the homeless, jobs for the jobless. We did not get these things but that did not stop these ambitious fellows from making new promises. I was waiting for them to promise wits for the witless."

Nimal said I would understand more about international aid if I watched elephants. We would go to Kandy, in the central part of the island, the next day to see what he meant. In Kandy, Nimal pointed out a Festival Elephant taking part in a Divali (Hindu Festival of Lights) celebration. In South Asia, you will often see Festival Elephants at such events and at elite *tamashas* or *durbars* (upscale parties). They get the attention of the crowd by wearing gorgeous and sensational outfits. The Festival Elephant I saw was heavily bejewelled with rouged eyes. He was wearing a richly caparisoned howdah set with brightly colored glass, and strings of electric lights. To entertain the crowd he was shaking his lights with increasing vigor. Having impressed the crowd, he then did not know what to do next. As the crowd grew restive, he seemed to think the answer was to prance up and down a lot while trumpeting loudly. The crowd moved on. The elephant started his routine all over again, making new overtures to another section of the crowd. Festival Elephants get upset if no one pays attention to them.

They promise to entertain by providing ever more dazzling acts, which everyone would like to see but which, at some point, the elephants cannot perform. Unfortunately, the Festival Elephants think that promising is the same thing as performing.

Poverty Close-up in Sri Lanka

In 1989, I became the director of a private-sector development project based in Colombo, Sri Lanka, funded by the United States Agency for International Development (USAID). President Premadasa had appealed to the U.S. government for assistance with a flashy private-sector initiative that would move the country from socialism to a market economy. Our USAID project, in contrast, lacked glitter. Instead, it was close to the people, it made sense on the ground, and it worked in many small ways. When I compared this project with the big poverty projects of other aid agencies, I was reminded of the Festival Elephant performance I had seen in Kandy.

Three years later, I had learned a good deal about the problems, aspirations, and capabilities of poor people in Sri Lanka. I began by initiating a country-wide baseline survey to find out about the lives and aspirations of "poor business people" I wanted to know what skills and knowledge they *had* rather than what they did *not have* in a material sense. Of course, the poor need money, food, education, and health care. But the material deprivation and degradation of their existence is not everything. In order to help the poor, it is necessary to know what they want and the extent to which they can help themselves with their own knowledge and social capital.

The project sent teams of researchers throughout the country to talk with poor people, listen to their ideas, and assess their resources for achieving a better life. Though this research took several months, it was essential if we were to be able to provide meaningful assistance. I wanted to know what poverty meant in the Sri Lankan context, because I had come across a variety of poverty in my earlier work. In the South Pacific, poverty could be a matter of being an unsuccessful fisherman, an albino, a woman left without a husband, or a farmer unable to grow decent-sized yams. In Tanzania, poverty was often a matter of not having kin.

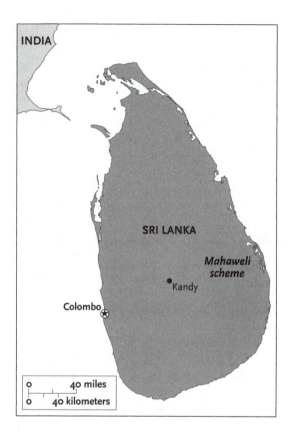

Our survey in Sri Lanka showed that people were poor because of social class and caste, religion, ethnicity, or gender. They were poor because they had no husband or children, or were landless or homeless, or had bad luck, or did too little to help themselves because of a belief that it was pointless to struggle against fate. Some were poor because they drank too much *arak*, or coconut toddy, which is as strong as rum. Some were mentally ill, some lazy, and some physically handicapped. Some people made a living by purposely appearing to be poor. Some ruthless people broke the limbs of young children and left them to heal in grotesque ways so that the children could earn money as beggars.

We also had to find out whether it was possible to work with and through the many small associations and trade groups. We learned that business people needed help in lobbying the government or otherwise dealing with its regulations. A businessperson who wanted to export a garment had to complete over 300 forms. Working closely with the Colombo Chamber of Commerce, the premier Chamber in the country, which was founded in 1840, we sponsored the establishment of local Chambers of Commerce outside Colombo.

In addition to doing baseline research on poverty and people's potential for change, I was convinced that it was essential to establish a social relationship between members of the project field teams and the people they wanted to help. In many development assistance situations, in contrast, experts stand back from the target population and rely on host country professionals to do much of the interpersonal work.

In Sri Lanka, poverty was like HIV/AIDS in that it produced a state of social disconnectedness for the afflicted individual. The more severe the poverty, the greater the social isolation. Such isolation could affect speech, diet, and personal hygiene. The extent to which a poor individual can get cut off from society was brought home to me in 1974 when I was working with USAID staff on the requirements of the "New Directions" Foreign Aid Legislation, which emphasized the need to get aid directly to the poorest people overseas.

In the late 1980s, staff inside the offices of the United States Agency for International Development in Washington, D.C., part of the U.S. State Department, worked on how to deliver aid to countries as varied as Mongolia and Peru.

Meanwhile, outside the State Department, on a hot air vent on 22nd street, was a man named Willy Dodds who neither local nor international development assistance personnel had been able to reach. He had been living on the hot air vent for about ten years. His shoes were stuffed with newspaper, his old army raincoat tied with string, his shopping cart tied to a lamp post. But he had heat during the long cold winter, and he had easy rummaging access to a garbage bin where office workers dumped breakfast and lunch leftovers. Staff entering and leaving the State Department building ignored Willy. It took me several months to be able to exchange a few words and learn his name. Salvation Army and Washington, D.C. City Government social workers offered him secure housing, better clothing, hot food and small amounts of money. But Willy would not take their help because none of it appealed to him and none of the helpers asked him what he wanted. Like many people confronted with a very poor indigent person, these office workers assumed that they knew what Willy needed. When pestered with offers of help, Willy pretended to be deaf and dumb. And if somebody passing by offered him money and told him to get a hot meal, Willy would look at his benefactor shyly and trundle off to buy cheap red wine at a liquor store a few blocks away.

It was not enough to design projects that spent millions in the hope that some of the money might end up helping poor Sri Lankan people. It was more important to aspire to partnership by trying to provide assistance that poor people wanted—assistance that recognized and involved poor people's values, knowledge, skills, and social capital.

The project began by giving small grants to business people in Colombo after we had gotten to know them and they us. We gave a grant of $200US to individual men and women who scavenged in the rubbish dumps of Colombo for aluminum cans to recycle. Through it, they were able to employ more staff to collect cans in hard to reach places. We also gave a few hundred dollars to the Maharagama Three Wheelers Association. These were rickshaw owners who wanted to employ an advocate to lobby the Colombo city authorities on their behalf for access to better parking.

Small business people wanted to know when they should try to expand and when they should sit tight. We helped these business people to construct a Business Confidence Index, and this was regularly circulated among members of the new small Chambers of Commerce. The Index was not based on high flying economics but on advice from small business people: if you want to know how well the economy is doing, you need to know how many bags of cement were being sold, or figures on the sales of electrical spare parts and sanitary napkins. We listened to small-scale gem merchants when they told us how difficult it was to market their artificial gems (they used kilns and very high temperatures to produce artificial rubies called *gauda*). When a deputation from the Colombo Chamber of Commerce came to the project for assistance, we quickly agreed to try to help them by sponsoring an international jewelry trade fair. They wanted, and they eventually got, overseas orders for their jewelry.

Nimal understood that the Festival Elephants of the aid world want to be involved in huge, flashy projects involving the glitter of millions of dollars. Over the life of the project, we had many visits from very senior international agency personnel who were interested in our approach to poverty alleviation through private sector development. Representatives of one international agency said that it was going to establish a global microfinance facility modelled on our grant giving. While they did not follow through, they and spokespersons of other aid agencies continued to put out press statements saying how they were going to win the War on Poverty by getting help to poor people. But they and their aid never got close to any poor people in Sri Lanka that we knew.

Festival Elephants on Parade

In 1984, while I was working in Papua New Guinea, the Finance Department in Port Moresby received a communication saying that a senior official from the World Bank wanted to visit. Puzzled, because the proposed trip would take place over the Easter holiday, the Ministry of Finance queried the dates. Back came an icy reply saying that the official would visit when the country was prepared to receive him. The Ministry of Finance straightened out the matter with the help of their Washington, D.C. embassy on the understanding that the Prime Minister would be in his office ready to receive the visitor when he arrived on Easter Sunday.

PNG finance officials were worried that this senior official would use the visit to point out what his institution could do for the poorest people in the country if only they would take more project loans. The official's job was to move more money to his client countries this year than he had moved last year. Senior officials persuaded countries to sign up to projects and programs, though the paperwork depended on consultants who could write nice project documents in order to get staff members through the bureaucratic hoops but did not know the countries. This process did a good deal for the aid agencies but little for poor people. Unfortunately, Papua New Guinea already had a number of project loans that had not delivered—indeed one project, the Agricultural Services project, was about to be cancelled. The Finance Ministry's query as to whether the visitor would like to hire a plane was rebuffed with the remark that simple travel was all that was wanted. The country went ahead and hired a plane at high expense for trips, figuring that anyone who made this much fuss probably wanted to be treated as important.

It is not only the very top officials who behave like this. Many visitors got quite angry if they did not get star treatment. Another senior official came from Washington, D.C., to Papua New Guinea and stamped about like a 5-year-old child because no minister had met him at the airport. When the Deputy Prime Minister and his colleagues met with the man, he sketched out some dazzling ideas that promised to transform the economy. When asked if he could help further, the official smiled winsomely and said he was really very busy with China. A senior economist announced he would like to visit the Secretary for Finance and arrived, despite having been told that his chosen time was inconvenient and that the Secretary for Finance would not be able to see him. The Secretary declined to cancel other appointments in order to see him. In retaliation, the man's boss complained to the Minister of Finance at the Annual IMF/World Bank meetings in Manila that the Secretary was wasting the time of his staff.

Festival Elephants who talk movingly about poverty have arranged their lives so that there is not much chance of encountering poor people. Those who say they want to help the poorest people have become part of the international diplomatic apparatus. UN agency representatives living in poor countries are accustomed to being treated as ambassadors. Many aid officials have offices in the embassies and lead the life of diplomats when overseas. Flags, limousines, communiqués, Foreign Ministries and ambassadors, international agreements, the Vienna Convention, immunities, inviolability and so on are part of the life of aid officials.

Festival Elephants talk about global problems rather than about the problems of poor people as understood through fieldwork and personal experience. They talk about the prudence and the discipline needed to defeat Global Poverty. They talk about the way to reach this ambitious goal, about instigating a new international trade regime, forgiving debt, sorting out the imperfections of the market, putting in place a sensible regulatory environment, providing good governance, and making an income or food security safety net available for all. You will hear that even if sufficient funds can be provided to eliminate poverty, there is still a great deal of work to be done to avoid "aid fatigue" and to persuade governments to show "commitment." The Festival Elephants will trumpet about the importance of primary education, and protecting the environment, and sustainability.

A new variety of Festival Elephants has recently emerged: rock stars and politicians who visit Africa or a disaster site for a day or two and then come up with the answer to the problems. Like the classic Festival Elephants, these new fly-in/fly-out Festival Elephants subscribe to the Myth of Global Poverty. They also promote solutions that are one-size-fits-all and involve shovelling more money in the direction of the illusory category of the global poor.

Office-Bound Festival Elephants

Seventy to ninety percent of the staff of global aid agencies and civil society organizations spend most of their working careers in large office buildings in New York, Washington, D.C., Geneva, London, and Paris. They process projects and loans, raise money and generate public support for their activities. Many reach senior positions without having lived and worked for lengthy periods in poor countries close to poor people. They make short trips to developing countries, but even then, most of their contacts are with senior government officials and consultants in the capital city.

In Rajasthan, India, I watched as a UN aid mission held an evening meeting with those they thought were the local opinion leaders. They suggested to the audience that local people needed the benefits from the global programs they had developed to supply clean water, primary education, birth control, and, of course, poverty alleviation. The meeting attendees did not disagree. When the mission members left to report to their headquarters, I stayed behind to talk with the women who were clearing up. Those who had attended the meeting didn't seem to be pleased with the outcome, and I asked why. Hadn't they agreed that what would be provided would be helpful? Eventually, they admitted that it didn't seem right to disagree with powerful people like those on the aid mission. What they had really hoped to get was a girl's toilet. At night, they had to send their young daughters a long way to the nearest latrine, and the girls were often molested on the journey.

Rich countries employ armies of social workers to work one-on-one with poor people. Global aid agencies and civil society organizations, in contrast, avoid hiring social workers, and their staff do not make house calls on the poor nor do they do meals on wheels. French or Spanish language skills are common among aid workers, but few have expertise in lesser-known languages. The Myth is sustained by experts in policy analysis whose context-free formulas supposedly fit anywhere and everywhere. So why pay attention to people in particular places and cultures?

While I was working in Washington, D.C., in the 1970s, the World Bank did away with loan officers—the person with on-the-ground community skills. Few of their successors could match their grasp of local languages or their extensive in-country experience. These were people who developed, or who already had, an in-depth knowledge of the country and its people. Most had lived and worked overseas for long periods of time. They provided integrity to the lending process and ensured that specialist staff paid attention to local factors. Moreover, they were very good at establishing relationships with a variety of people in poor countries, and were thus in a good position to know what poverty was and what, realistically, could be done about it.

Specialists in tropical agriculture and other technical fields, who, like loan officers, also had developed hands-on skills, disappeared. Most global aid agencies thought it impractical to maintain and keep up-to-date all the specialized technical and cross-cultural knowledge that their activities might need. Instead, they emptied out their organizations of its technical expertise, replacing the specialists with managers who were responsible for finding consultants with the required knowledge and skills.

This change resulted in situations where millions and millions of dollars have been spent without anyone in the organization experienced enough to know if the money was spent wisely. Tree crops, livestock, and health were handled without agencies having top in-house expertise in these areas. Civil services were reformed by aid agencies without anyone who had ever worked in a civil service. As time passed, staff had less and less relevant experience and substantive knowledge with which to make sure that the thousands of consultants who did much of the basic work on the ground were doing a good job.

In addition to the thousands of staff at aid agency headquarters, an invisible auxiliary army of hundreds, probably thousands, of accountants and economists are employed by such big international consulting firms as Arthur Andersen, KPMG, Deloitte, and Touche Ross. It is these consultants who process a growing pile of the paperwork needed to spend the money raised on behalf of the Myth of Global Poverty.

Festival Elephants Raise Money for Festival Elephants

Raising funds for the War on Poverty has become more and more time-consuming as the global aid institutions have become "alms dealers." Instead of working to help the poor help themselves, they have moved toward giving alms to the poor, and thereby upstaging faith organizations. As a result, giving alms to the poor, a religious practice for Muslims and Christians, has been secularized and globalized by aid agencies and civil society aid organizations. UN offices in Washington, D.C., New York, and Geneva are now counting houses as they continue to appeal for and receive more and more money.

Development assistance provides around $50 billion U.S. dollars per year to poor countries, with the intention of eliminating half the world's poverty by 2015. Aid agencies have lobbied the governments of wealthy countries to double this amount to $100 billion a year to ensure that their poverty reduction goal will be achieved. In 2003, the rich countries were a net taker of funds from the poor countries to the tune of over $20 billion. This negative transfer is not new. During the 1970s and 1980s, there were many years during which the World Bank received more money in loan paybacks than it disbursed in new loans.

The ever-growing numbers of staff hired to work on the new Global Poverty programs are good at processing paper and putting out publications that touch the heart strings and show the importance of the Myth. More and more, children feature in fund raising literature because the plight of children touches most people and because children are especially vulnerable—hit by malnutrition and illness just when their brains and bodies are forming. Some 160 million children are moderately or severely malnourished (as of 2007). Some 110 million are out of school. Women in poor communities are particularly at risk for disease and death. Half a million women in poor countries die each year in childbirth—at rates 10 to 100 times those in industrial countries. They are burdened by the strains of work, the birth and care of children, and other household and community responsibilities. Their lack of access to land, credit, and secure employment opportunities handicaps their ability to fend off poverty for themselves and their families, much less to rise out of poverty.

The facts and figures about Global Poverty cited in these agency publications are usually sound and impressive, believable to the point where the average reasonable person feels outrage at the situation and demands an immediate solution. The proposed solutions focus on the problem and on exactly what will do the trick in an economical and quick manner: provide oral rehydration kits, engineer boreholes, or distribute tree seedlings or seeds for food crops. It is impossible to judge if any of these approaches makes a difference to poor people on the ground without fine-grained project evaluation studies. Just showing that the aid agencies raised and spent a certain amount of money is insufficient.

In the War on Poverty, the pen has proved much mightier than the sword. Those with good presentation skills are promoted. Many of those who have risen to senior positions have a background in journalism. What a strange war. Imagine a war led by generals who have never been soldiers, and navies being commanded by admirals who have never been sailors. But they can write inspiring text for lavishly illustrated brochures.

Peter McGinty had been a financial journalist with the Belfast Telegraph in Northern Ireland before he joined the United Nations Development Programme in New York as a Program Officer (a professional level P5 post in the UN personnel system). In Ireland, he had specialized in writing about childhood poverty and trauma as a result of "the troubles" between Catholics and Protestants. At the UN he advised poor countries about social security for children. He rose steadily through the ranks, moving quickly to D1 and then D2 UN diplomatic grade. He was able to take aid agency jargon and translate it into powerful messages about poor people written in simple English. Although, as part of his job, Peter wrote a great deal about the poverty challenges posed by Africa, his on the ground experience was limited to a few pleasant months spent as a student in Malawi.

While his masters at the UN lurked in the photographic fringes of G7 economic meetings of the major industrialized countries, Peter gave papers on poverty at international conferences and made sure that what he said was noticed by them and quoted. Development assistance was evolving into a media event in the industrialized countries, and a clever person such as Peter could manage the media to the advantage of both the UN and himself. Peter was not averse to letting it be known that he was Irish because it avoided any colonialist taint. It was also a useful card to play in the UN where nationality had a great deal to do with who got top jobs.

On one occasion, when his wife's yuppie New York friends came to dinner, they talked well into the night about his job. They were curious how people in the UN, like Peter, who had never had anything to do with poverty on a personal level, could hope to have an impact on reducing poverty around the world. Peter made deprecating gestures and replied that it was not the job of people like him to work with poor people. Instead, he explained, the UN has a unique ability to create the conditions that make it possible for others to do this work.

The wine-infused guests challenged Peter on this point. They simply did not think it possible that forty or fifty thousand UN staff like Peter, working on poverty alleviation, would be able to facilitate the elimination of poverty in the world. World poverty elimination was not a bureaucratic process that could succeed if managed by bureaucrats. They pointed out, further, that mass poverty alleviation could not be defined as the UN agencies did, as an economic or a human rights problem. Instead, mass poverty alleviation was a political and religious issue, and the UN was out of its depth in these areas. As the guests drank a couple more bottles of good Bordeaux, they went on to argue that doing away with poverty would require world revolution. How else could one make sure that the rich gave the poor their due? The social forces that would have to be harnessed by the UN to eliminate poverty would require an emotional propellant or an ideological commitment similar to that seen at the origin of the Christian and Muslim faiths or the birth of socialism. But the UN relied on capitalist methods, and history shows that capitalism widens the gap between the rich and poor. Surely the UN was naive if it maintained that getting the policies right and increasing their budgets would do the job! Where was the ideology that would stir the masses? World poverty elimination would need scores of leaders with the gifts of a Nyerere, a Gandhi, or a Kemal Ataturk. Where were the Third World champions? Would the UN produce Third World champions? The UN could not even produce its own champions.

It was a bruising evening, both to Peter's self esteem and his wine.

Worker Elephants: No Glitter

In Sri Lanka, those who want to get a job done well look for a Worker Elephant. Worker Elephants, unlike Festival Elephants, do not have big egos or big ideas or a big opinion of themselves. They don't prance and shake their bells and then leave. They do small things well. They have staying power. They succeed by being good team players and good communicators. In the Mahaweli region of Sri Lanka, my friend Nimal had seen Worker Elephants get together to flatten an electrified fence. One group of elephants got timber and pushed down the fence, while others put logs on top of the flattened wire. Then the herd passed safely to better pasture. Worker Elephants are patient animals that take the time and the trouble to get to know what works and what does not.

For a Worker Elephant seeking to alleviate poverty, the most important activity might be a task where there was no supervisor, no paper trail, no prospect of a reward: an agronomist visits a remote farm or village, spending time with those who need help; a teacher goes out of her way to help a pupil who was not in her class; an accountant, given tax receipts to review, increases a refund because the tax payer had made an arithmetical error, though nobody would know what she or he had done. Extra effort was not only vital; it was the very substance of a sense of service.

After being trained in social anthropology at Oxford, I spent my first two years as an Administrative Officer of the British government in the Solomon Islands trying to understand village society. Language skills were important. You were on probation until you had passed exams in the local language (in my case, Pidgin English), and the exams were not easy. A colleague said to me: "People will come to you with complaints. You must know enough of the language to grasp what some toothless septuagenarian, spitting betel nut juice at your feet and waving an axe, is saying. You must also be able to convey the government's concerns about young men who think they can bite off some person's nose just because he or she is from another island. And if you want people to think you understand village society, you must be able to tell a joke that makes people laugh."

Like many young men from a privileged background who joined development aid agencies, I thought I knew something about poverty. I assumed that poor people would be like everyone else if they had more money, which was something I could help them with. I changed my mind in the Solomon Islands. While working there, I once saw a hideously deformed man—a leper—approaching me as I stood in a jungle clearing. I remember wondering, at the time, if the leper's fingers would come off if I shook his hand or if I would contract leprosy. I had been told that the lepers did not trust outsiders, and did not want to be "found." Forced to live as social outcasts, they had no way of earning money. Nonetheless, I assumed that the lepers would want money to buy store goods such as clothing or an axe. I was wrong. They wanted tobacco and salt. Later, when I looked back at this incident, I felt ashamed of being afraid and of the fact that I just wanted to shove help at the lepers and keep my distance.

Fieldwork and participant observation, which I had been taught to do while at Oxford, confirmed the fact that culture provided the essential glue that bound members of society together. Culture animated the social relationships between members of society that persisted through time. Anthropologists celebrated cultural difference, the distinct cultural heritage of each society, by showing how each society had unique features. They were able to show that, far from being pre-scientific, magic, witchcraft, taboos, and sacrifices had their uses. Culture was not a constraint. It offered an explanation as to how the world started and humankind developed. It provided the basis for law and order and governance. It offered hope that danger and threats could be managed, that crops would grow, and that disaster could be kept at bay.

In the 1950s and 1960s, it was customary for people working in international aid to emphasize the importance of cultural competence, as part of what Ambassador Harlan Cleveland, distinguished American diplomat and academic, called *overseasmanship skills*. By this term, he meant that working overseas required special competencies in much the same way as sailing requires seamanship. Social or cultural anthropology played an important role in the European colonies starting around the turn of the twentieth century because of its attention to overseasmanship skills. At that time and for several decades following, colonial anthropologists did more than just provide information to policy makers. They shaped policy. For example, anthropologists inspired the important policy of Indirect Rule, which said that the colonial powers should work with and through traditional leaders.

Goals for development assistance were shaped by the assessments of these field personnel as to what the colonial government could and could not do in terms of change and how long change would take. Most of the colonial government personnel were in "the field" rather than being in London or Paris or Washington, D.C. The small number of experts at the center was responsible for developing policy and providing technical backup in areas such as agriculture or medicine. Most of these people had grassroots experience in one or more developing countries.

Training a Worker Elephant in the Later Twentieth Century

In the 1960s, young graduates in the United States, Britain, and continental Europe who wanted a career in developing countries as an administrator, agriculturalist, business executive, doctor, educationalist, forester, missionary, or military professional were trained to ensure that they had the capacity for understanding and working with people of other cultures. The training aimed to give recruits the ability and confidence to think for themselves and to realize that they could be facing situations never previously encountered in which no global cookbook solution would be of use. Training emphasized the importance of local languages, local culture, and local knowledge. The field of cultural anthropology helped these practitioners to question, within particular cultural contexts, the idea that Western-designed change would necessarily be a good thing for local people.

Those recruited for work in developing countries were exposed to the history and culture of the countries. In Britain, they were then sent to the field to acquire hands-on skills that would enable them to engage successfully with local people. To do this they needed to understand local society and customs, in order to earn local trust and respect. They were tested at the end of their three-year probationary period. They were given formal exams in criminal law, Colonial Regulations, and local administrative rules called General Orders. When their appointments were confirmed, they then spent twenty or thirty years in developing countries, living away from London and its amenities. In Britain, the top universities (Cambridge and Oxford) offered courses for colonial administrators-to-be. I went through such training at Oxford and then joined the Overseas Civil Service in 1962.

Trained as a Worker Elephant, I signed on with the Overseas Civil Service at the close of the era when Worker Elephants were valued.

Within a few years of my appointment, those in charge of the British government's bilateral aid became so enamored of the approaches and models of the World Bank and the United Nations that it soon abandoned the hands-on community training and activities of its field staff. By the 1970s, the Worker Elephant, community-level tradition was so completely expunged, that the British government had difficulty in finding knowledgeable administrators to run its remaining embarrassments: Gibraltar, the Falklands, and the Virgin and Cayman Islands.

In 1973, while teaching anthropology in the United States, I was invited by Bernard Chadenet and Warren Baum of the Central Projects Division of the World Bank to assess how it could use social/cultural anthropology. Together with my graduate student, Raymond Noronha, I examined Bank projects in agriculture, health, education, transportation, and tourism to see what contribution might be made by anthropology. Bank staff members such as Francis Lethem, Martijn Paijmans, Stokes Tolbert, and Albert Waterston provided very valuable advice, as did the World Bank's first Environmental Advisor, Jim Lee. When we submitted our report in 1973, there were no professional anthropologists on the Bank staff. Within two years, Raymond Noronha and a Romanian sociologist, Michael Cernea, were hired. As of 2007, the Bank employed about 100 full-time cultural anthropologists (several of the early hires have now retired, including Noronha and Cernea).

In the 1970s and even now, many World Bank staff thought that involving an anthropologist on a project would result in complications and delays. Ambitious project managers want to avoid complication and delay. The anthropologists hired were not used to working in large-scale, highly politicized institutions, and they lacked tough bureaucratic skills. They were not always able to access resources or gain policy influence. Few had training which enabled them to work with economists, the major players in development policy and programs. As a result of these factors, anthropologists became identified with constraints on projects rather than with how to make projects work.

I, along with others, was more successful in having an effect on the United States Agency for International Development (USAID), the

U.S. bilateral aid agency. In the early 1970s, Jonathan Silverstone and Ed Cohn of USAID's Policy, Programming and Coordination Division, and I developed *Social Soundness Analysis*, an appraisal system for development projects that included attention to the local cultural landscape in project design and implementation. Social Soundness Analysis became a required procedure in USAID. In the next few years, USAID hired around twenty-five anthropologists as full time staff. This was a period when USAID's stated objectives were to help the poor and when it was far more open to input from cultural anthropology than it appears to be now (2007).

Through the efforts of Dan Creedon, head of USAID's Manpower Development and Training Division, the Development Studies Program, a multidisciplinary training program for USAID field staff, was launched in 1974. I designed and delivered the anthropology content. Richard Gable, from UCLA, Don Warwick from Harvard, Richard Blue from the University of Minnesota, Jim Weaver from American University, and Albert Waterston who had just retired as the World Bank's Chief Planner, developed the public administration, political science, and economics content. In its thirty years of operation, the course exposed hundreds of USAID field personnel to the role that could be played by anthropology in development and to the importance of interdisciplinary perspectives. Such efforts, however, proved to be the exception rather than the rule.

The Myth of Global Poverty Entrenched

The Myth of Global Poverty now dominates global aid agencies. It has been a growing trend since the 1980s. These organizations, with their hundreds of millions of dollars, have moved aid away from valuing local cultural knowledge in development projects and policy.

Today, poor countries are host to more and more Festival Elephants. The Myth of Global Poverty and the growth in global programs have enabled aid agencies to become ever more powerful global political institutions. The World Bank's staff of four hundred or so in the late 1960s has grown to around 13,000 (in 2007), most of whom live and work in Washington, D.C.

Poverty not only continues to exist but it is increasing, in both absolute and relative terms, in many parts of the world. Festival Elephants and their institutions are also growing. While they claim to help the poor, they do not listen to and answer to the needs of poor people. Yet they go on prancing and dancing. The accountability of these large global institutions is weak because they have access to cheap money, backed by rich country governments, from the bond market, and because they answer to diplomats from member countries in the UN General Assembly and a few legislators who, in many instances, are not very knowledgeable about aid matters.

Staff with cultural competence that is based on many years of working in developing countries have been squeezed out of the global aid agencies like toothpaste from a tube. Whereas in colonial times, anthropology was considered a key discipline in the design and delivery of development assistance, the emergence of the Myth of Global Poverty as a universal and monolithic entity and the introduction of global programs changed all that. Cultural expertise was replaced by safeguard functions, such as making sure resettlement was properly handled or that acquired land for agricultural development had a registered title. Even though anthropologists were on staff in the World Bank and USAID, they had limited influence on policy and performance. Instead, the universalizing fields of economics and accounting rose to the top, displacing local, contextualized expertise.

Worker Elephants in an Unlikely Place

I rediscovered Worker Elephants when I went to work in community relations for Rio Tinto in 1995 (Chapter 6). I found that some people in the mining industry wanted to learn what poor people could do to help themselves. Many of these companies spent substantial amounts of time in the field getting to know local people, their aspirations, and their abilities. They were motivated not by the rhetoric of humanitarian aid, but by the objective of extracting resources and returning a profit for the company—goals that are best achieved by avoiding harm to local people. The best companies in the mining industry increasingly realized that they had to take local people into account, and they had to learn to work with them on their own terms.

Like my colleagues in the Solomon Islands in the 1960s (Chapter 3), many of Rio Tinto's mining staff were not office-bound. They spent long periods of time in the fields, got to know local people, and had a feel for local realities. Outside a mining camp at Cerro Colorado in Panama, I saw a mining engineer look at how the local Indians had strung wire on their fence post. He remarked on how tightly the wire had been strung—not an easy thing to do. This emphasis on what poor people *could do* to help themselves rather than what they *did not have* in terms of income or education was a step in the right direction.

Reading

Cleveland, Harlan, and Gerard Mangone. 1957. The Art of Overseasmanship. Syracuse: Syracuse University Press.

Cochrane, Glynn. 1974. What Can Anthropology Do for Development? Finance and Development 11(2):20–23.

___. 1979. The Cultural Appraisal of Development Projects. New York: Praeger.

Cochrane, Glynn, and Raymond Noronha. 1973. A Report with Recommendations on the Use of Anthropology in Project Operations of the World Bank Group. Washington, D.C.: The World Bank, Central Projects Division.

Hancock, Graham. 1989. The Lords of Poverty: The Power, Prestige, and Corruption of the International Aid Business. New York: Atlantic Monthly Press.

Merry, Sally Engle. 2006. Human Rights and Gender Violence: Translating International Law into Local Justice. Chicago: University of Chicago Press.

United Nations. Human Development Report (annual). New York: Oxford University Press.

World Bank. World Development Report (annual). Washington, D.C.: World Bank.

3

୬ୢ

A Worker Elephant Apprenticeship in the Solomon Islands

My High Commissioner in the Solomon Islands, somewhat irreverently, did not believe that anyone in London could know what was best for the Solomon Islands. How could someone who had never been to the Solomons have anything definitive to say about their future?

One Sunday morning, when I was the Duty Officer at the Western Pacific High Commission Secretariat in the Solomon Islands, a long, complicated cipher communication came in. When decoded, the cable described revisions to British government thinking on the New Hebrides, an island condominium, or joint territory, of France and Britain, and advice for us on how to promote these changes during an upcoming visit to the New Hebrides by General de Gaulle. I rushed the cable to the High Commissioner, who was completely unruffled and unexcited by it. After asking me how long I had been on his staff, he then advised me not to take messages from London too seriously: "Sometimes London makes quite good policy, yes quite good, but sometimes not so good policy. However, you must always remember there is no need to worry as long as I am here." He saw London as a junior partner and one whose actions required close scrutiny. I was learning.

I joined Her Majesty's Overseas Civil Service (HMOCS) in 1961 as one of the last six career ("permanent and pensionable") officers appointed. I was trained at Oxford University in social anthropology, British law, tropical agriculture and forestry, development

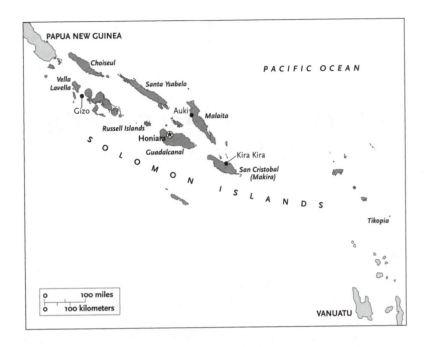

economics, local government, field engineering (how to build offices and clinics and court houses), and the history and culture of the Solomon Islands. I learned the Gilbertese language, now called Kiribati.

When I arrived at my post in the Solomon Islands, I was appointed as Magistrate, Justice of the Peace, and one of Her Britannic Majesty's Deputy Commissioners for the Western Pacific. As Magistrate, I heard criminal and civil court cases brought by the police, and either dismissed the charges or complaints or imposed fines, prison sentences, or damages. As Justice of the Peace, my role was to perform marriages and to deal with unusual deaths in much the same way as coroners did at home. As Deputy Commissioner, I had labor market functions and was concerned with overseeing any recruitment of Solomon Islanders to ensure that labor laws were followed. As an administrative officer cadet, I served as a District Officer for four years before becoming District Commissioner Eastern.

The Solomon Islands became a British Protectorate at the end of the nineteenth century after local people murdered and ate several missionaries. The twentieth century brought more rapid contact with the outside world, especially during World War II. After exposure to the War's heavy fighting between U.S. and Japanese forces, and the frequent arrival of ships and airplanes full of astonishing material goods, Solomon Islanders decided that the wealth of the outsiders must be the result of their access to the cargo that arrived from overseas. Following this logic, local people developed rituals, called Cargo Cults, as a way for them to get access to cargo or Western material goods. They would sometimes prepare a long table set for guests, or simply stand in quasi-military formation, waiting for days for the cargo to arrive. The cargo did not appear, but cult leaders worked hard to keep people's beliefs alive. Colonial officers and Christian missionaries, thinking they could discredit the leaders of the cults, told the cult members that it was silly to wait so long for a dream to come true. The cult members responded by pointing out that Christians had been waiting 2,000 years for Jesus Christ to return.

At the time of my appointment, the Solomon Islands had a population of almost 300,000 people. The protectorate was divided into four districts: Malaita; Central District, which contained Guadalcanal and the Russell Islands; Western District, which contained Gizo, Choiseul, Santa Ysabela, and Vella Lavella; Eastern District, which contained San Cristobal, Ugi, Ulawa, and the Polynesian island of Tikopia. Each District was administered by a district commissioner who was assisted by two or three district officers. In addition, each district usually had expatriates serving as agricultural officers, education officers, forestry officers, and engineers in the public works department, fisheries officers, cooperative society officers, medical officers, and police officers.

The High Commissioner for the Western Pacific administered the Anglo-French Condominium of the New Hebrides, as well as the Gilbert and Ellice Islands Colony and the British Solomon Islands Protectorate. He had a Secretariat in Honiara on the island of Guadalcanal. Sir David Clive Crosbie Trench, the High Commissioner, later Governor and Commander-in-Chief of Hong Kong, had served his time in the field and knew pretty well what could and could not be done. Despite its small size, the Solomon Islands proved to be a good training ground for Hong Kong, because that was also a place where getting things done was important. The Chief Secretary I worked for in the Solomon Islands went on to become Colonial Secretary in Hong Kong and the Financial Secretary in the Solomon Islands went on to head the government department responsible for housing in Hong Kong.

Officers in the Western Pacific High Commission were supposed to be able to work well both in the Secretariat and in the field. Although the system relied on a certain amount of creative tension between field and center, it also relied on their cooperation. The Secretariat would never embark on a new course of action that had implications for district administration unless there had been extensive consultation between all concerned. In fact, both secretariat and field officers were able to make a useful contribution only when they were aware of each other's strengths and weaknesses.

Any official writing to the Western Pacific High Commission had to send two copies of their letter. One copy was immediately put in a folder and circulated to all officers in the Secretariat. Senior officers would often write comments in the margins about which file the memo or letter should end up in, on whose desk, or who should deal with the matter and what was known about it. When incoming correspondence was received, it was registered in the incoming correspondence register with notes about when the correspondence was received and how it was filed. It was thus, in theory, practically impossible to lose a piece of correspondence. When the appropriate file for incoming correspondence was located, the item was placed in the file and the file was sent to the officer who was expected to take action. All files were kept in a file registry. As each file was sent from the registry, the front of the file was marked to show who received the file. Files might then be marked as they went from officer to officer. The file would contain all previous letters and memos. A minute sheet, attached to the inside of the top cover, was used to make comments as the file went from office to office. Finally, when a reply had been drafted, and approved in the case of important issues, the reply would be issued from the Secretariat and an entry made in the outward correspondence register.

A letter from the public was to be answered within two weeks and if this could not be done, an interim reply had to be sent, stating the reason for the delay and when a final answer could be expected. Confidential letters were to be sent marked "confidential" but then enclosed in a plain envelope. Letters from the Chief Secretary or anyone on his behalf had to end, "I Have the Honor to be, Sir, Your Most Humble and Obedient Servant." Such a letter would go to a villager in the remote bush in response to a query about the payment of a government tax or a firearms license.

Local people found the High Commissioner difficult to understand. His formal dress may have had something to do with it. Our civil uniform consisted of a pith helmet, a short gilt sword, a white tropical tunic with gold buttons, and gorgets (black velvet tabs with embroidered insignia, denoting rank) attached to the neck of the tunic. My High Commissioner had all this plus an impressive plumed hat. While wonderful for photographs, it did not impress local people. I once asked a Solomon Islander if he had seen the High Commissioner, who was supposedly attending the Queen's Birthday ceremony. I said in Pidgin English: "you lukim Big Man b'long me fella?" ("Have you seen my High Commissioner?"). He replied: "Me lukim, hem he wok long Mrs Kween ("I saw him he works for the Queen"). Hem he long fella man too much ("He is a very tall man"), an on top b'long head b'long hem ("and on top of his head") e gottem ogleta fetha b'long arse b'long kokerok" ("and on the top of his head he is wearing feathers from the backside of a chicken").

I accompanied the High Commissioner to the formal opening of a local garage that sold new cars and trucks. After thanking the High Commissioner profusely for coming, the owner turned to me and said that everyone had grown to admire the way I made a public convenience of myself. The suggestion that I was doing the job of a public toilet, it seemed to me, very aptly described the way both my employers and Solomon Islanders regarded my job.

At the time, I was learning just how different life in the tropics could be compared to living in Britain. Meat and fish were not regularly available because there was a shortage of refrigeration. There was no milk because there were no cows. Each day, the temperature was in the nineties, with humidity that always seemed to be around a hundred percent. As a result, I spent the day perspiring and my clothes were never dry. Everything had mildew. Letters disintegrated. Cameras had to be packed in tins full of silica gel. There were no faxes or computers; if I wanted to copy anything I might be allowed to use something called a thermo fax. When outside Honiara, electricity was available only from two to four hours a day. Government quarters had refrigerators but they were powered by kerosene, not electricity, and occasionally had to be turned upside down to ensure that they got cold. White short-sleeved shirts and white shorts with long white knee-length socks were worn in the office. If I attended a formal event in the evening, I wore what was called "red sea rig": dress trousers and shoes, and a short-sleeved white shirt with a cummerbund.

I had to learn how to get things done in a government bureaucracy. This required lots of experience, good judgment, shrewd assessment of people, patience in negotiation with people from all walks of life, and an intimate knowledge of the bureaucratic entrails of government. Then, using all that, it was necessary to interpret and fashion colonial regulations and policies to fit with villagers' culture and aspirations. Quite frequently, visiting experts would suggest a good idea to do this or that. But no matter how brilliant the suggestion, it had to get through bureaucratic hoops and past people who could think of little else other than putting bureaucratic hoops in your way. Rules that civil servants had to follow in contacts with the public were laid down in General Orders. Government Telegraph Code (GTC) was used when sending confidential news of promotions, civil disturbances, or anything that little old ladies and gentlemen on plantations that spent their days monitoring government radio were not supposed to hear. The GTC, which had been around in hot spots of the British Empire for a long time, used messages made up entirely of five-letter groups. Many of the groups had been formed during more stirring days of the Empire. Examples of groups that could be used included some that said: "Should I open fire after reading the Riot Act?" or, "Reinforcements on their way," or "the bridge has been blown-up."

It was not enough to have a nice vision about helping people. The hard work, the most important work, was mastering all the detailed arrangements that implementation required. I learned early on that to do a new project, I needed help from somebody who knew the colonial bureaucratic system, somebody who could help with hiring and purchasing, and all the other things that could come back to bite you if you got them wrong. On one occasion, a friend of mine, an officer, purchased a tanker full of diesel because he knew the station was running out and there would not be a ship for another few months. As the purchase was not in the budget, my friend was charged with the cost of the fuel. He told the financial secretary that he would be happy to pay off the bill government had given him, but when the station ran out of fuel, as it would in a few days, he was prepared to sell to government at double the price he had paid.

Another office who had to handle a resettlement following the destruction of houses by a cyclone found that he had to make a number of expenditures that were not in the budget. He eventually found himself charged by the auditors with a bill that was ten times his annual salary. He told me he wasn't going to worry about the surcharge because it was so big they would work out a way to forget it. It was much more dangerous to get a small surcharge that they could recover, as I found out after a £3 surcharge was taken out of my salary.

In 1965, Harry Chapman, a British executive officer from Newcastle, England, was about to leave the Solomon Islands because he was fed up with his job as an advisor on privatization. A few weeks previously, Harry had burned his bridges with the Advisor from London over debt collection. The Advisor, against Harry's advice, had persuaded the secretary to advertise for a number of debt collectors. When no responses had arrived, Harry had taken great delight in pointing out that nobody who knew the first thing about business in the country would advertise for a "debt collector;" what you advertised for was a "junior accountant." Harry did, and got 200 applications.

One of Harry's British friends, Benjamin Middleton, who worked in the Treasury, asked if the arrangement he had made to destroy old bank notes were all right. "How will you actually destroy the money?" asked

Harry. "Well," said Benjamin, "I'll be the presiding officer. We have to shred all the money and then we have to burn it. We are going to do 10 million. Should take only a couple of hours, right?"

Harry beamed fondly at the twirling stem of his wineglass. "You may be a little late for your golf game. I helped to write the currency legislation, and I stipulated that the Presiding Officer had to record the number of each note destroyed."

My training in cultural anthropology (or social anthropology in Britain) helped me to understand an initiation ceremony I saw in a forest clearing when I visited the New Hebrides (now called Vanuatu). It was a ceremony that inspired what is now known as the sport of bungee jumping. The people had built tall towers from massive timbers, with the old men of the community supervising the construction. At the time of the ceremony, the initiates climbed to the top of the towers. Strong vines were tied to their ankles. Bird-like cries came from the initiates as they leapt high in the air and swooped down hundreds of feet to the ground. Such was the skill with which the towers had been erected and the vines selected and tied that the initiates fell so close to the ground that their hair brushed the forest floor. The ceremony served several functions. Successful jumpers became men and the ceremony strengthened the community by validating the importance of elder men. It also guaranteed the fertility of the season's yams.

In the Solomons, I discovered that big ideas, without cultural understanding, could be embarrassing. Following the advice of the World Health Authority, I had several maternity clinics built. But the clinics were not used. I asked a Catholic priest who had lived in the area for some time if he could explain this irrational attitude. He told me there was not a woman on the island of San Cristobal who had not committed adultery. According to local cultural rules, a woman going into labor had to say out loud the name of the baby's father. If they failed to do so, they would be taken by a shark while bathing in the sea. Apparently sharks were great upholders of family values. Eventually, I found and hired nurses from Fiji who had little interest in village adultery.

Women began to use the clinics. The anthropologically informed view shows that Solomon Islanders do not see things the same way as bureaucrats in London do. While London thinks, "Build a clinic and they will come," the San Cristobal women think about sharks.

Law and Order and Local Government

Magistrates had to be careful, when they tried to apply British notions of crime and punishment, to make sure that they had understood the local cultural context. At Malu'u, in the north of the island of Malaita, police found a number of torsos without heads. The bodies were found on the mainland just opposite a series of artificial islands that had been built in the lagoon. When I saw the bodies, it was clear that the heads had been severed from the bodies by a sharp instrument such as an axe. Mortuary practices on the island involved burial with the head protruding from the ground. When the flesh disappeared, the heads were placed in a skull house for worship. Police were sure that these funeral rituals had no connection with the headless bodies.

Harvey Hudson had a plate in the back of his head, the result of having part of his skull blown away at Monte Cassino during the Italian Campaign in World War II. He had been due to read Natural Sciences at Cambridge but the war put an end to that. He was a very rich man in his own right and had assumed what seemed to some to be rather foppish ways. For example, most of the food he ate came from Fortnum and Mason in London, and he employed more servants than the Chief Secretary.

The Chief Justice of the Western Pacific High Commission did not like him. When he set Harvey Hudson's law exams, he set a question asking what offense would be committed if someone let the air out of a car tire. Conduct likely to lead to a breach of the peace? The victimization went on, or so it seemed to Harvey Hudson. "He has quashed me again," he said wearily as he glared at the order from the Clerk of the High Court Chief Justice, setting aside the verdict he had given in a rape case some weeks earlier. The Chief Justice said Hudson had been wrong in his assessment of the age of the accused, who had been charged with unlawful carnal knowledge of an underage girl. Apparently, the Chief Justice, who had just come from Hong Kong, thought everyone in the Solomon Islands ought to have a birth certificate. Because the local penal code was silent on the matter, the Chief Justice said that Hudson should have followed the laws of England. Hudson thought it would be idiotic to apply English law. Young men and women were sexually active much earlier in the tropics than they were in Britain at that time. The prosecution in the case had said, "em he gottem grass," which meant the accused had hair under his arms and must be a teenager; therefore the accused was guilty.

Priding himself on his thoroughness, Hudson had even asked the accused if he was born at the time of the great cyclone—a date that everyone knew—and the fact that he said he had been a young boy at the time of the cyclone clinched it for Hudson. Under the laws of England, a young man up to the age of 24 could claim that he didn't know the real age of a female minor and might well get away with it; in the islands, that kind of claim would never wash. Hudson thumbed through his well-worn copy of Archbold's Criminal Pleading, Evidence and Practice. Nothing. Not surprising since things were not the same in Sussex.

Harvey suspected the Chief Justice of having a hand in the disastrous decision (disastrous to Harvey, that was) to make adultery a civil offense after it had been seen as a criminal offense for many years. Students of jurisprudence told us that, in theory, a criminal offense was one that offended most people in society and for that reason adultery was a criminal offense.

Another problem with the Chief Justice followed. He quashed Harvey's conviction of two young men for the locally known offence of "creeping," Creeping occurred when young men climbed coconut trees at night in order to see into the lighted bedrooms of women. Naturally, as Harvey Hudson pointed out to his friends after the Chief Justice quashed that verdict; "creeping" was not in his copy of Archbold which usually had the answer for everything a magistrate needed to know. Anyway, as a matter of principle, Harvey Hudson appealed the "creeping" case reversal to the

Chief Secretary, thinking that he might tell the Chief Justice to ease up a bit. Back came a one-liner: "The Chief Justice's decision shall be construed as he intended." Shortly afterwards, Harvey Hudson was in deep water again. As magistrate, he had conducted a preliminary enquiry into a murder case in which the accused had aimed a shotgun at a man he suspected of having sexual relations with his daughter. He discharged the weapon and killed the man. The police had introduced the heart of the victim as evidence. As the presiding magistrate, Harvey ordered the heart to be marked for identification as an exhibit. Adjourning the court, due to the lateness of the hour, Harvey forgot the heart and went to the club. As he was starting on another delightfully cold beer, a policeman arrived and told him that the heart had been eaten by a dog.

With the benefit of hindsight, I realize that our attempt to build local government institutions was probably the most important thing we did. Local government was the first step on the road to nation-building. After strong local institutions had taken hold, the intention was to then focus on the national level. If you look at former British colonies, you will often find that it is at the local level that the most lasting and most useful contribution was made.

I regularly visited local government clerks to check the books and help them with letters and bank reconciliation. We helped councils with their projected revenue and expenditure for the next financial year. Councils were shown how to work out what to charge for services because they needed to tap all their possible sources of revenue. A thirty- to fifty-year timetable made sense because change had to be accomplished slowly over a period of years, rather than in a dramatic and sudden way. The Gilbertese people, who we resettled in the Solomon Islands, had an expression, "teutana i mwin teutana," meaning that change was like drawing a canoe up on the beach. You cannot pull a canoe all the way up the beach all at once; you have to pull it up bit by bit. Similarly, building local government in the Solomon Islands was not dramatic. It was nuts-and-bolts work that had to be repeated and repeated and repeated, slow step by slow step.

Parliamentary procedures were gradually introduced. Emphasis was placed on getting the basics right: making sure taxes were collected and putting sensible budgets and byelaws in place. Local government dealt with quite small, but important, things that were close to the people. It taught people how to work as an elected group. Local people needed time to grasp the difference between being a delegate and passing on views from home and being a representative with the ability to make independent decisions.

Finding a good leader was important. Government tried to get the "Big Men" to play a key role in the councils because they were superb leaders. They knew how to encourage, guide, prod, and lead their people; and they could encourage their followers to consider the poor. Councils passed resolutions about witchcraft; draconian laws were discussed for adultery; playing cards could be outlawed; support for a prominent citizen who became president of the council could result in a decision to commit virtually all the money in the treasury to the man's salary. Officers learned to accept the often odd decisions of local authorities, drawing the line when it looked as if fairly fundamental human rights were about to be breached.

The trick with local government was to ensure that it did not simply reflect narrow community opinion. To work, local government needed a broader contribution. A great deal of local knowledge was required to draw local government boundaries. Boundaries that were too close to clan lines and the Council would simply reflect existing social arrangements. Boundaries that were too far from clan boundaries and local people would not develop a sense of ownership, and they might not work well together.

Officers also spent large amounts of time getting a slate of good councilors elected, then slowly teaching them to take responsibility for various functions, helping them to work out the costs of local government, and to augment the grant monies that central government gave them. They also taught the public what to look for in the people they voted for. I helped fledgling politicians write their speeches, choose the symbols for their political parties, and watched the "whispering ballot" (because voters who couldn't read or write whispered the name of their candidate into the ear of a polling assistant). In later years, politicians who had learned their trade in local government provided the basis for the parliamentary institutions that emerged with independence. Politics produced leaders—not always ones we liked—but finding leaders was essential.

The tragedy of the Solomon Islands was micro-nationalism. The country did not hang together, which has caused the country to experience terrible law and order problems in the last twenty years. Islanders did not think of the Solomon Islands as a nation. While this did not affect local government, it did have a negative effect on the building of national institutions. A person from the island of Makira, or Owa Raha, or Ugi, would have a sense of kinship for others from the same place, provided the island was not very large like Guadalcanal or Malaita. But when he encountered those from other islands, there was often hostility rather than bonding. Local government institutions were developed for each island. Prominent local citizens occupied the positions of president, clerk, or treasurer. Other prominent citizens were elected as members of the council. Consequently, local government was well understood and well accepted, but its capacity varied greatly from island to island. This unevenness had to be accepted because councils were usually reluctant to have outsiders fill important posts.

Poverty in the Solomon Islands

London viewed local government as having a key role in taking care of poverty. There was no way we would have thought we could have eliminated poverty. We could help to control poverty, we could curtail it, but we thought it would always be with us. We didn't spend our time looking for poor people to help, though we did try to help those who were very poor indeed. At the time, London was more concerned with economic development than poverty alleviation. However, with respect to poverty alleviation, we looked to local government. As at home in the U.K., we believed that it was at the local government and community level that the poverty of the individual had to be defined and understood.

In Solomon Island communities, poverty was a matter of being unable to play one's social part. Within the family, it meant being unable to act as a father or mother, unable to help sisters, brothers, and kin with important obligations they incurred as they grew up, married, and had children. For villages with a strong hunting tradition, it meant being unable to hunt or perform as a warrior, unable to work hard and well in the garden. In fishing communities, it might mean being unable to swim underwater or being afraid of stingrays or barracuda.

Most Solomon Island communities would include, in their listing of people who were poor, pedophiles and the mentally ill, as well as those who were physically handicapped or without close kin, and thus unable to secure a daily living on their own. Poor eyesight or hearing or a cleft palate affected the ability of the individual to feed a family. There were special instances of poverty, as was the case with men and women suffering from leprosy or yaws (a disease that causes deep putrefying wounds in the body). Albinos—some communities could have a high proportion of albinos in their population—were also considered to be poor people. It was difficult for them to garden, hunt, or fish because they could not tolerate long exposure to sunlight.

Local government was ideally placed to know who was very poor. They could not only help poor people but also encourage the very poor to not be too afraid to seek help. The Red Cross supplied prosthetic devices; many of the missions did what they could to supply clothing and food. Poor people in the Solomon Islands were spread out, one in a village here, another in a village there, and they often wanted to be left alone. We encouraged councils to report instances of severe poverty but Solomon Islanders did not see poverty alleviation as the business of government. Various types of poverty were seen as involuntary afflictions; something that nobody would choose of their own volition. Villagers did not blame pedophiles; they simply watched them and made sure that they could cause no harm. The community acted as a corrective institution in the case of the mentally ill. The entire community, young and old, took on these responsibilities collectively. Local solutions to poverty were sometimes brutal. Solomon Islanders often thought that old people were so close to death that a little push was warranted. There were reports of poor old people being buried alive.

Nobody in the village would fake poverty because he or she would be exposed to shame. Nobody could shirk his or her duty to the poor because that would be shaming. Being shamed in a community was the ultimate form of social control and often led to suicide. Young girls who became pregnant and shamed by their kinsmen would often commit suicide; young boys who failed to meet the test of manhood did the same. In one case of suicide, a man who broke wind in front of his chief was so ashamed that he climbed to the top of a coconut tree and killed himself by sitting on the hard spathe. In the Solomons, as elsewhere in the South Pacific, suicide is often the only path to honor.

Such local perceptions of poverty and social failure and how to deal with them could in no meaningful way be captured in an economic equation or reduced to figures in an accountant's ledger. Similarly, poverty, as lived and experienced in the Solomons in the 1960s, could not be eradicated by a plan hatched in London, Paris, or Washington, D.C., informed only by economic equations and disbursing more loans.

Fieldwork in the Bush

A strange shooting party I attended while I was living at Kira Kira helped me begin to understand a little more about cargo cult thinking. Harry Waro, a friend who had relatives on a small island about twenty miles out to sea, asked me to go and shoot pigeons that were destroying the islanders' crops. When we arrived, I had a twelve bore shotgun and assumed that there were no other firearms on the island. No, said Harry. His relative, who had an old World War II U.S. carbine, would come and shoot with us. Harry pointed up in the trees at a pigeon and told his relative to fire. The relative pointed the gun, shook it a little, and said "boom." The man was sure that he was shooting. I realized that cargo cults might be similar: If cult members observed and then went through the right motions, then, logically, cargo should come to them.

Since the 1990s, cultural anthropology has woken up to the fact that learning about culture in a globally connected world requires more than spending a year or two in one village or on one island. So-called *multi-sited research* became in vogue in cultural anthropology in the 1990s.

It means that the anthropologist, while situated mainly in one research location, also spends time doing research in other areas in order to get a wider view of variation across localities and of local-regional-global connections. My years of combining my official role with research in the Solomons were, thus, an early form of multi-sited research. I was officially based in Kira Kira, one of four stations in the Solomons. The others were at Auki on Malaita Island, and Honiara and Gizo in the western Solomons. I also spent substantial amounts of time moving about in an area of up to 25,000 square miles at sea and several hundred miles on land. At the time, my "multi-sited research" as conducted outside the district stations was called "doing a tour." My duties as an administrative officer required me to spend fifteen days a month on tour. Officers drawn from the agriculture, education, public works, police, and cooperative departments would often accompany me. Junior officials from the District Office also came on tour because we would hear court cases and collect taxes. We inspected schools and hospitals to make sure that they had adequate supplies. We listened to any and all complaints from the local people.

Tours through the thick tropical jungle were on foot; those by sea took place on a 60- to 70-foot wooden-hulled craft that stopped at various small government centers. When touring by ship, officers headed to previously announced destinations on the coast, so that those who wanted to discuss, complain, or explore ideas were free to gather about.

I didn't enjoy malaria or the awful seasickness that was an inevitable accompaniment to inter-island travel. I learned that coconut juice stains a white shirt, and I cannot forget how strong the smell of a rotting sago palm can be. But touring was the only way to listen to the people and get to know them. Officers who thought that they could wait in their offices for callers soon acquired a very bad reputation.

Walking along the beach was no easier than trying to go through the jungle because the soft sand was ankle deep and sand flies nibbled the legs, and the reflected glare of the sun made your head ache. We could see crocodiles running down the banks of the rivers we had to cross. My small party usually made rafts from their knapsacks and tried to gradually work through the current in order to land up somewhere further downstream but, we hoped, on the other side.

In a village perched on a high mountain in the center of the island, I met a retired cannibal. He had lived in this part of the jungle on the island of Malaita for many years. When he was a very young man, his kinsmen had been captured by slavers, or "Blackbirders" as they were known, to work on the Queensland cane fields. It would have been more accurate for him to say that he had sold them into slavery, since he showed me the gold sovereigns he received for his treachery. He said that he had killed the Blackbirders after they set up camp on shore to try to get more slaves. The Blackbirders' heads were bashed open, their throats cut, and the blood carefully collected to make puddings. This was also the custom with pigs. Indeed, a couple of the Europeans were cooked like pigs. Their body hair was singed off over a fire and then their bodies were put on the hot coals. Two other Europeans got the Cordon Bleu treatment. People dug pits and lit fires that burned until there were plenty of embers. They placed rocks on top of the embers. When the rocks were very hot, they were covered with banana leaves. The bodies came next, topped off with more banana leaves and held down by large logs. People poured water over it all, making a sort of steam cooker. Unfortunately, even this sophisticated cooking method failed to make the Europeans good to eat. They were too salty. The retired cannibal said that normally the best part is the palm of the hand.

Villages both in the bush and on the coast were small, seldom having more than 100 to 200 people. At the top of hills in the jungle there was no water for drinking, washing, or cooking. Water had to be carried in bamboos from the river or stream below. A short journey on the map was an entirely different matter on foot. Even though inhabitants of one village could call to the inhabitants of another village, walking between them was an arduous task. It was necessary to descend 1,000 to 2,000 feet of sheer jungle, slipping and sliding in the red mud, ford a river or stream at the bottom, then scramble vertically through bush, to emerge panting, perspiration-soaked and thirsty at the other village. Bamboos were not always filled with water. In one remote area that had not been visited by an administrative officer for a long time, I was encouraged by the hospitable villagers to swig down the contents of the bamboo, only to realize I was drinking liquid pig fat.

The jungle canopy was so thick that little daylight filtered through. After you had gone up a couple of thousand feet, scrambling up red mud banks, and pushing through thorny bushes, you got very thirsty. At the top of the big mountains was a small pile of stones. Men who felt good after the steep climb put a pebble on the pile; I didn't.

We stayed for two or three days in order to have news of our arrival and availability passed to distant villages. Local headmen would arrange for us to talk to village groups about possible development projects, such as growing more tree crops for export sales. We held meetings with the village people at night, because during the day, most adults would be away working in their gardens. In the bush, a touring party would walk for seven or eight hours during the day and then sleep in a leaf house, which was usually the men's house in the village and as such vacant. The following day, we moved on. No official "rest houses" existed, as in other parts of the British colonies, such as India. Sometimes we would walk for five or six days to emerge on the coast and be picked up by ship and taken back to district headquarters.

The heart of the tour process was sitting down and listening to all sorts of people, men and women, of different ages. Some had advice or queries. Some were angry and wanted to complain. The sessions revealed what people thought and wanted. I learned what hard work it was to listen. Listening was not just hearing; it was also the ability to understand nuances and cues as well as accompanying body language. It also included the ability to sort out truth from performance. Being kind and polite people, the villagers would often tell me what (I think) they thought I wanted to hear. In addition, I learned how unwise it was to rely on the views of just one or two individuals. Even more complicated was the need to try to work out why a particular person had certain views as compared to someone else. As the Solomon Islanders began to rework the colonial services into their cultural objectives, many became increasingly adept at telling the kind of story that would work best to enhance their political strategies. They learned about us while we learned about them.

Touring enabled me, and those who accompanied me, to develop a solid baseline understanding of the district, its economy and society, its potential for change. I could see where roads might be sited, where there was good unused land, and where wharves might be built to help get agricultural produce to market. I also wanted to learn if there were health problems that warranted the building of clinics. Similarly, were children able to get to a school without having to walk too far? And, importantly, what did the local people see as their major problems and needs? At the same time, I paid attention to the Solomon people's own capacities and knowledge. They possessed all the local knowledge; we colonialists had very little of that. Instead, we had knowledge of the outside world and its interests.

On the basis of many and repeated local stays, my colleagues and I were in an informed position to make proposals to Honiara and to London for the funds and assistance that new initiatives would require. We undertook no new initiatives unless the villagers had thoroughly discussed them and agreed to them.

Through the tour process, I established and maintained relationships with a wide variety of people throughout the district. They got to know me and I got to know them. I could talk with them. I knew their names, their problems, their strengths. The network of village headmen helped me build and sustain relationships throughout the region. The British government appointed these people on the basis of their respect and trust among the local people.

Land

As a government officer, one of my duties was to purchase land for roads, airfields, and housing around outstations. While buying land may sound like a relatively simple matter, it definitely was not so in the Solomons at that time. Solomon Islanders had a strong bond with their land. In the many local languages, the word for land is the same as that for placenta. The depth of feeling was quite apparent if the British government tried to buy land outright. Europeans were killed who tried to acquire land or whose land dealings were suspect. Even just trying to rent land was difficult.

Landholders possessed highly advanced commercial instincts and determination to invent ways of gaining monetary compensation for their land. When I went to discuss compensation for a certain piece of land, I learned that the stands of coconut and breadfruit trees on it had amazing fecundity and, therefore, high monetary value. Another time, while arranging compensation for land to be used for the construction of an airfield, I saw local people at the site at night burying the bones of an animal to establish a basis for lodging a fairly substantial claim. The Solomon Islanders had a culturally built-in sense for capitalism in the form of land compensation.

When trying to assess the availability of land for cash cropping (growing crops for sale to the market rather than for their own use), my training in anthropology alerted me to the likelihood that Solomon Islanders might not see things the same way as London did. On one occasion, I asked why we were having trouble doing land surveys in a remote part of Santa Cruz. On the island of Malaita, I learned that Solomon Islanders did not see their land as Westerners do, like a box with four sides. They defined their land with reference to an ancestral shrine built at the center. This concept made sense in a tropical rain forest environment because the undergrowth was very thick. Conventional boundaries would have been impossible to establish and maintain. Knowing that people defined their land by its center and then cultivated in a circular fashion around that shrine would help avoid conflict. When surveyors and geologists arrived from England and started making measurements without this local knowledge, problems arose because they had assumed that the Solomon Islanders' concept of local land boundaries was the same as theirs.

In order to be able to mortgage land to get a bank loan—and Solomon Islanders wanted to raise money with their land—it had to be professionally surveyed and registered in the name of the owner. But in the Solomon Islands, as in many other countries, vast areas of land had not been surveyed and registered. There was also an extreme shortage of surveyors. Beyond that, the culture of people's relationship to the land added several layers of complexity not to mention equity issues. I was never very enthusiastic about land registration because it wasn't fair to all the traditional owners. Whereas individuals in industrialized countries can sell or dispose of their interest in land, the individual in many traditional societies has no identifiable estate but is more like a shareholder (in anthropological terms, a co-parcener). Thus, land ownership, or the closest one might get to a Western concept of it, was vested in a lineage, clan, or other social group that might have 100 or more members. Any transaction would have to be understood and agreed by all members of the social group. Other complications arose. If a woman was pregnant, the unborn child had interests. Even the dead might on occasion be considered to have ownership rights. And the dead, being the most senior generation in many societies, were likely to have objected to selling the land or any other kinds of change affecting the land.

I spent a great deal of time listening to land cases that were always about who the real owner was. When we introduced cash crops such as copra and cocoa, flat land near the sea became a contested resource because villagers wanted to grow these new crops. Land cases were time-consuming. First, I listened to the plaintiff and the defendant reciting all their ancestors who had lived on the land. This was a bit like listening to the Book of *Genesis* being read out loud, because getting to the original (apical) ancestor involved going back twelve or thirteen generations. Then, I walked the "spearline" or boundary of the piece of land in question. Finally, I had to weigh the merits of the plaintiff and the defendant, and give a judgment. In giving judgment, I called on respected local people, called "assessors" to give their views.

Health

As a government officer, I also learned about health problems and, with this knowledge, helped promote programs to improve health. The most common ailments were skin diseases, malaria, and respiratory diseases such as tuberculosis, which at the time posed a serious threat. I spent a great deal of time while on tour trying to reduce the amount of standing water in communities in order to eliminate breeding places for the carrier of malaria—the mosquito. We encouraged villagers to cut down undergrowth in order to expose the village environment to the wind, and we talked constantly about the times when mosquitoes were most likely to bite. We tried to introduce mosquito nets, but they were never popular because people considered them hot and awkward to use. Spraying houses to kill mosquitoes was also unpopular. When the World Health Organization started a spraying program, it was rapidly met with disfavor—the reason for which involves several related factors. Small lizards that lived in the houses ate the mosquitoes infected with DDT spray. Cats that were kept as household pets then ate the lizards; those same cats developed fatal central nervous system reactions to the DDT. The villagers said they did not want any more spraying programs.

Chewing betel nut, the seed of the betel palm (*Areca catechu*), is a popular activity in the Solomons. People chew these small nuts along with lime made from coral and certain leaves that have a peppery taste. The chewing, along with saliva, produces a vivid red paste that is then spit out. Over time, with continued use, the lime paste turns teeth black, rots gums, and causes dental decay and cancer of the mouth. Those who chewed betel often loaned each other the little gourds in which they stored their lime. In this way, they unwittingly passed tuberculosis to each other. Trying to get people to stop chewing betel would have been like getting Americans to stop watching television. Knowing that, we tried instead to convince people to spit outdoors because the ultraviolet rays of the sun killed the TB virus.

Like people everywhere, Solomon Islanders wanted medicines and cures that had visible results. For example, penicillin was a successful treatment for skin diseases. Anti-malarial tablets alleviated malaria. In time, therefore, anyone who visited a clinic or hospital wanted an injection or some pills. Bandages and ointments were less popular.

It was difficult, however, to persuade people to invest time and effort in preventive health measures. What was particularly worrying was the fact that in some of the poorest communities, there was a reluctance to take sick children or old people to a clinic or hospital, particularly if the facility was some distance away. Few doctors, however, wanted large numbers of patients—each one arrived with ten or twenty relatives who camped outside the clinic and needed to be fed, sometimes for months on end.

Social Relationships

An essential part of my job was to establish and maintain relationships with people throughout the district: leaders and followers, men and women, old and young. My anthropology training, which had taught me to respect people and value their views, helped me to get close to people. I got to know many people in the Solomons, including those who lived in the deep bush by the coasts and were called by all Solomon Islanders "saltwater" people, and those who became involved in the administration in district headquarters and in Honiara. I learned that, while important differences existed among individuals and across communities, most Solomon Islanders shared similar notions about power and status, and similar ideas about what is the sacred and what is profane.

It was easy to establish relationships with Solomon Islanders because they thought (rightly so) that they were as good as anyone else. They welcomed me and others in the administration as people of interest and potential value to them. They had no notion of inferiority in their relationships with colonial officers. (In 1927, the people of Malaita hacked to death two administrative officers who had offended them.) I noticed that the expatriates who successfully established and maintained local relationships often did so because they had good manners that translated well into good manners as defined in the Solomons. They listened, were concerned about others, and they kept their word.

My anthropology training and language skills, however, were not enough to prepare me for the complexities of social respect in the Solomons, as in the rest of Melanesia (the region in the South Pacific that stretches from the western part of what is now Indonesia through Papua New Guinea and the Solomon Islands to Vanuatu). People in the Solomons have their own ideas about respect, fairness, and retribution when needed. My colleagues and I had to walk a fine line between being too soft and too hard, and that line had to be informed by local ideas. For example, during World War II, the Solomon Islanders labeled Americans as *picininns*, the pidgin term for children, implying that they were easy targets for their goods. At the same time, local people hated the tough Australian planters because they treated Solomon Islanders like *rubbish men*, the pidgin term for people of no value. I had to learn their terms of reference for what was right and good, and how to become part of their culture of exchange and interaction.

What did Solomon Islanders make of us? Certainly, from the perspective of a Solomon Islander, we British were distinctly odd and not very human. We stayed for a few years in the islands, went away, and did not come back. We did not marry local women or live with them since London strongly discouraged liaisons between staff—who were male—and Solomon Island women. We did not go to the gardens in the mornings to work. We did not sit down to chat and chew betel nut. We did not have anything much to do with births, deaths, and marriages other than to register the fact that these things had happened. Nor were we like the missionaries or the planters, who spent their lives in the bush.

They wondered: How could I work for the Queen and not live in her house or in her village? How could I want to be seen as an important person when I didn't grow very good yams, wasn't very good at spearing fish or catching shark, wasn't a particularly good orator, had no pigs or shell money for a respectable bride price, and hadn't given any big feasts? Not surprisingly, the Solomon Islanders did not copy my dress, food habits, or much at all about the way I lived. The British administration had remarkably little impact on the Solomon Islanders' daily lives. The Solomon Islanders had cultural confidence, then.

How was I to understand Solomon Islanders? At home in Great Britain, if I wanted to know how to treat someone or how to get along with them, I had a lot of clues: their job, their school, their university, their clothes, their car, their house. Check out the data, slot the individual in place, and that was that. In terms of understanding the social position of a Solomon Islander, it was pointless to ask where they went to school, what their job was, what kind of car they drove, or even their favorite book, film, or radio program. Looking for commonality even in such a basic topic as food didn't help much either, as Solomon Islanders seemed to regard eating as a necessary but not very enjoyable activity, and certainly not worth discussing. Chatting about pets didn't work either. Dogs were kept to hunt in the bush. When I suggested to people in one village that it was time to pay the local government dog tax, they hanged every dog in the village.

Other misunderstandings involved mundane matters such as travel time from one place to another. Once, tiring of a long slog through the bush, I asked my companions how long until we reached the next village. "Oh, about two hours," he said. Four hours later, I asked why we had not reached the village and why his estimate was wrong. "Oh, I meant by bicycle," he replied. On another occasion I was taken a day out of my way because my companions wanted me to see a man who they said had such a small penis that they didn't think he would have been able to father the children he had. When we arrived at the village—and before I knew their reason for such a detour—they arranged for the man to come swimming with us so that we could see him naked.

Who was having sex with whom was a constant source of speculation. And stories could be checked because Solomon Islanders did not like to have sex in the dark at night. They preferred to go to their gardens during the daytime.

Over time, I learned to pick up on local gossip. This way, I found out who had the best yams, who was planting new coconuts, and when the Chinese businessman would come to collect the *copra* (dried coconut meat). I listened to what people were saying about each other: Was a certain young man keen on a certain young girl? How many puddings (dense mixtures of coconut and yam) had been given at the feast?

In the process, I had many aimless conversations. They were important precisely because they were aimless, casual, and therefore friendly. Building solid and sincere relationships cannot be done if the only time people see you occurs when you want something from them. I could get small things done by listening to local people and learning from them. These small tasks, like building a road or a wharf, increasing local agricultural production, improving public health, or making sure teachers could teach, depended on local people knowing me. In turn, helping a local council with a small tomato-growing project, or building a water tank, was an essential prelude to accomplishing larger initiatives.

Forging Partnerships

It is an ethical challenge to build and maintain a partnership if one side has substantially more power and resources than the other. Ideally, the power roles between the two parties are somewhat balanced, even though interests in the outcome may differ. No matter what, however, a partnership is, and must be, a social relationship. As anthropologists have documented from their studies in cultures around the world, enduring social relationships involve some sort of reasonably balanced understanding and exchange. One side gives and one receives, and vice-versa.

I didn't start out with this attitude toward partnership. Before I went to the Solomon Islands in 1962, I had been told by a British Ministry of Overseas Development official that I would be a change agent, helping the local people to a better life—an idea that the Solomon Islanders found tiresome. They made it clear that they expected me to serve their interests as well as those of the government in London.

In terms of economic development, Solomon Islanders brought much more to the table than we did. Economic development would not take place unless they contributed their brains and brawn. And we had to understand that the local economy would probably be a bit different than other economies. Before colonialism, the Solomons, like the rest of the South Pacific, were a non-monetized society. Items of high value included certain kinds of shells, pigs, and other objects that one could trade in order to create social ties and gain status. I became aware of what Western economists call the "elasticity of demand." Coming from the West, I had assumed that people in the Solomons would welcome the opportunity to make money. I was wrong. I was deluded by ethnocentric views that emanate from my capitalist culture that spurs us on to produce more, want more, and trade more. My culture was extremely concerned with getting "more." In the Solomons, in contrast, a man would work to earn money to buy batteries for a radio, a package of shotgun shells, or a bicycle. Once he had enough money to do that, he stopped trying to make more money. Needs or wants were not infinite as they were in the West. They were finite and achievable.

I also erred in thinking that village people had a great deal of spare time and that one only had to come up with a good idea about how they could use their "spare" time more "efficiently" so that they could make money and therefore get ahead, succeed. Once again, I was viewing the situation from my cultural perspective. Instead, I learned to ask what social (not to mention environmental) effects a new crop would have. What activity would people have to give up or curtail in order to devote time to growing these new cash crops and making money? Also, further down the line, if local people got involved in this activity, did it entail a steady demand of their time or only at certain times of the year? Did the activity involve both men and women? What would happen if the innovation failed? Villagers with limited resources with which to feed their families knew that a wrong decision might mean starvation. Starvation was not a possibility for me. It was for them.

It was important to develop a profile, or set of baseline information, about the people who could participate in any economic initiative that was offered to local communities. There was no point promoting development that called for literacy when many poor people were illiterate. Nor was there any point calling for volunteers from a landless area, for a project that needed several hectares of flat ground. Without baseline information, it was senseless for people sitting in offices in Honiara or elsewhere to design plans to help poor people who live in particular contexts. One had to get to know the people, listen to them, and then try to design something that would help as many people as possible.

The Local Economy and the Challenge of Money

When I was in the Solomons, some cash crops had been established. The main cash crops were copra, cocoa, crayfish, timber, *beche-de-mer* (flesh of sea slugs), exotic sea shells such as Gloria Maris, and timber. Copra and cocoa production required substantial amounts of land, and most of the land suitable for coconuts was limited to a narrow coastal strip around the islands. It was extremely difficult to find cash crops suitable for those living in the high bush. Crops such as cardamom and tobacco were tried from time to time, but they never took hold.

Copra production provides a useful illustration of the problems that Western economic development could bring. To an agricultural aid officer, it was important that the ground be properly cleared and that coconut trees planted in a 27-foot triangle, because experience showed that that spacing gave the maximum yield. But to a Solomon Islander, planting coconuts in this way meant that one had to do a lot of work to keep the coconut paddock free of shrubs and small trees. Moreover, one had to wait seven years from the time the nuts were planted until the first harvesting. Instead of planting trees in a 27-foot triangle, the Solomon Islanders preferred to plant them close together. That meant that there was a smaller yield than produced by the 27-foot scheme, but the nuts were easier to collect and the area that had to be kept clear was smaller. The ability to grow a cash crop that would suffer a fair degree of neglect was a good deal more important than many of our agronomists realized. Growing coffee was popular because it could be neglected yet produce berries and cash when needed. However, growing tea, which needed regular attention, was much less popular throughout Melanesia.

Administrative officers understood that they had an obligation to at least try to ensure that the gap between the able and the poorest did not widen. In the Solomon Islanders' view, wealth was a collective asset—something to be shared with the community, rather than a private asset to be consumed by the individual. Poverty was seen as a community responsibility. For us, a focus on community was important because we needed to know what was happening to local society. Did the individualism associated with economic development mean that the community was breaking down? Money made from selling cash crops often had a corrosive effect on relationships. Individuals making money became unwilling to share the proceeds with their kin in accordance with tradition. Were people cooperating or stealing from each other? Were they settling old grudges or looking forward? How willing were individuals to work for the common good? Would they work with each other, share with each other, help each other?

I had to appraise applications to the Agricultural and Industrial Loans Board. The Board made loans to farmers in order to plant cash crops; it also made loans to small business enterprises. We would go to inspect the farms of all borrowers and potential borrowers. We would trudge through the bush to distant farms, climbing over giant logs, pushing through streams, clambering through mud. On arrival, we would talk to the farmer and look at how well his existing crops were handled. We needed to know how the man would live for the five to seven years it would take for tree crops to be produced. Did he have other means of support? We wanted to be sure that the loan funds would be applied to the project the applicant had specified in his loan application. Sometimes loan funds might end up being spent on brideprice (money and goods that a groom and his family provide to the bride's family upon marriage) or on community wide feasts. It was also necessary to make sure that the farmer knew that we would return to make sure that everything was all right. If the loan were for a store, we would look at the books. We would show the storekeepers who did not know how, to do double-entry bookkeeping. Some books showed very high profits, but the sums were due from those who would not pay, or from relatives, who often felt that they did not need to pay. It was important to examine the actual cash in hand, or money that the trader could call on.

Simply increasing the amount of money people had could have negative effects. People unfamiliar with money and the wage economy fell into debt very quickly. They were used to growing or securing their food on an as-needed basis. Furthermore, Western money is owned by an individual, not the family or wider social grouping. In the traditional economic system of the Solomons, resources are communally owned and communally shared. In terms of development projects in this context, I found that it was more appropriate to consider a project that had communal benefits, such as a health center, a water supply system, or a generator.

There was no way that older people could make money. They lacked the energy to grow cash crops and they could not go to other islands to work as plantation laborers. Their inability to make money eventually came to be held against them by the young men and women who could make money, and who therefore began to think that they had the right to change society. I heard young educated men refer to their elders as "kumara tops" (tops of sweet potato, usually fed to pigs). Although the frustration of young, educated people was understandable, so too was the difficult position of their elders.

When an entrepreneur was thought to be acting in an antisocial manner, he could not expect to be able to call on help from his neighbors in time of emergency. For example, Joe Konihaka was wealthy in money terms because he did not share his affluence with his community or his kinsmen. Joe had bought an old expatriate's plantation and had replanted with fast-growing, high-yielding Malayan dwarf coconuts. He also owned a small boat that he used for inter-island trade. Joe didn't employ his relatives, but men from other islands; he didn't lend his relatives money. Most of his kinsmen didn't have a good word to say about Joe because he didn't play his social part. When a hurricane flattened his plantation and sank his ship, nobody went to his aid.

Earning money was not as important as having the traditional status of a "Big Man." Big Men used traditional forms of wealth that consisted of long strings, or "fathoms" as they were called, of small shells, through which holes had been painstakingly, and very cleverly, bored. The shell wealth was buried until it was needed—which was also what often happened to currency. Traditional shell wealth was used for brideprice, land purchase, and payment of compensation.

Young men who were ambitious and who wanted to earn the status of leader or "Big Man" could do so by engaging in competitive feasting. Aspiring leaders had to work very hard to take care of their family obligations while also helping other men. When they judged that they had a sufficient number of men who were indebted, they would arrange for a feast using food that was paid back. On one occasion I estimated that the cost of the food that had been donated to the feast was several thousands of pounds. The next day, the new leader came to see me to borrow the price of a packet of cigarettes. He was happy, had lots of status, but no money. Big Men bought trucks, boats, and large machines for the use of their followers. These assets would be unusable a few months later since the primary purpose, conspicuous consumption, had been achieved. Maintenance of plants and equipment was somewhat alien to Melanesians.

Disaster Relief and Resettlement

Tsunami occurred frequently because the Solomon Islands are located in a region of strong seismic activity. Fortunately, big surprises were not common because Solomon Islanders listened to their radios and benefitted from good early warning systems. Villagers looked out for telltale signs of freak wave activity and made for high ground when the signs were dangerous. This method didn't always work: After one violent earthquake, I found flattened villages and survivors lashed to trees—most of them with broken limbs. I remember that even though most people wanted fresh water, there were also many requests for underwear. However, a few months later, we returned to see houses that had been built in the same dangerous places.

Tikopia, a small Polynesian island that, as District Commissioner Eastern, I was responsible for, suffered a terrible cyclone attack in 1966. The first radio reports suggested that all the inhabitants, as well as those living on nearby islands, might have been wiped out. As District Commissioner Eastern, stationed at Kira Kira on San Cristobal in the Solomon Islands, I was expected to help. Fortunately, I had spent substantial amounts of time visiting Tikopia. In addition, we had a blueprint for emergency relief thanks to the work of the British anthropologist Raymond Firth. He had written six major books about the island, including one dealing with the problem of famine. (I brought Firth back from Tikopia to Kira Kira in 1966, following his last visit.) So relief was not too difficult to organize and deliver.

I knew that there were no people living on Fataka. It is a place where men from Anuta go to collect bird's eggs, a fact which I knew from having rescued one of the two chiefs, or Ariki, from the island when a storm swept away his canoe. On a previous visit to Tikopia, the Ariki gave me an exquisitely carved traditional fishhook for the Queen. The Tikopia Ariki had wanted the Queen to know they existed and that she should look after them. I helped to arrange for the gift to be sent to London to the Victoria and Albert Museum. I knew the four Ariki on Tikopia. I knew about the water supplies on Tikopia, and their caves and other places that might have kept them safe. I knew the food stores they would have had on hand, how much food the entire island consumed, and what would have happened to the food in the ground in their gardens. I knew how much seed they would need to replant and how long it would take to replace food supplies. I knew how their houses were constructed and what sorts of materials, and what sorts of quantities, would be needed to restore these structures. I knew how the men of the island could be organized and what danger there was of stealing or looting as food became scarce.

If you look closely at a map of the central Pacific Ocean, you may find the Phoenix Islands. I was in charge of resettling all the people who used to live in the Phoenix Islands to the western Solomon Islands in the early 1960s. The Phoenix Islands had received no rain for almost seven years. The coconut trees were dying and wells produced only brackish water. Indeed, one of the remarkable things about the young children there was that they had never tasted fresh water. The authorities were carting water by ship at about eight knots to the Phoenix group from Tarawa, thousands of miles away. The Phoenix Islands consisted of low coral atolls. It was said the islanders would get vertigo if they got 15 feet above the ground. Agriculture was hard work. Only a few vegetables could be grown; pits that had to be dug and filled with compost. Fishing was a major activity. Money had been earned from copra production and also from working heavy machinery in connection with the phosphate industry on Ocean Island. Others had worked on the Christmas Islands when Britain was doing atomic testing between 1952 and 1967.

In order to move the Phoenix Islanders, the government established a resettlement team to do the job. Each member of the team spoke Gilbertese. Some were from the Solomon Islands and some were from the Gilbert and Ellice Islands Colony, of which the Phoenix Islands were a part. The first task of the resettlement team, which contained marine, health, and agricultural personnel, was to visit the Phoenix group to get the permission of the islanders to move. Once this was done, the team began to survey the existing way of life of the Phoenix Islanders as a prelude to designing their reception in the Solomon Islands.

There were three main communities containing, in all, about 1,100 people: Orono, Nikumaroro, and Kukutin. Two main religious groups were represented: the London Missionary Society and the Roman Catholics. The resettlement had to be organized by community because, due to religious differences, the two communities would not work together. Even the dancing was different between the Catholics and the London Missionary Society. Catholic women danced bare-breasted with a movement of the hips known as "washing-machine action." London Missionary Society dancing was much more restrained.

When the settlers, and their canoes, arrived by ship at Wagina Island in the Manning Straits of the western Solomon Islands, the resettlement team faced several challenges. Malaria had to be controlled. How did one ensure that 1,000 people who were not used to popping pills engaged in regular prophylaxis? We distributed mosquito nets but people used them to make women's underwear. We had to watch visitors who arrived by canoe at odd times and in odd places on Wagina from Bougainville or Choiseul. Many of these visitors were malaria carriers. In fact, the settlers did fine; I was the only one who caught malaria. One or two people did swallow several hundred antimalarial pills at a time but it didn't seem to do them any lasting harm.

Public health professionals told me it was important, when building latrines, to find out if people were sitters or squatters because motor functions are not easy to change. Unfortunately, as far as I was concerned, all this was shrouded in a certain amount of secrecy. I eventually concluded that Gilbertese were standers. We built latrines over the reef and covered the sides of the structures with coconut fronds for privacy. The Gilbertese removed and reused all the fronds and resisted replacements because, more than privacy, they valued conversing with those on the platform or on shore while they performed their bodily functions.

Settlers began to build houses, but both house construction in the Solomon Islands and the materials used were not familiar to the Gilbertese. We arranged for a team of Solomon Islanders to come from Choiseul to show the settlers how to make houses the local way, using local materials. In the Gilberts, coconut fronds were used to roof houses, but these roofs lasted only for three years or so. Solomon Islanders used Nipa palm rather than coconut, which lasted for five or six years. The timber, which was used as house poles in the Solomon Islands, was different and so was the trunk of the betel nut tree, which was used for flooring. Nails were used in house construction by Solomon Islanders rather than the sinnet cord made from coconut fiber used in the Phoenix Islands. The Gilbertese were slow and methodical. They insisted that the floors were absolutely level. The house posts had to be well seated. The roof had to be carefully put on. We had estimated two months for house construction, but it took almost six months.

Around 400 acres were made available to the settlers, which, when added to the other suitable ground, meant that each family was to be allotted around 10 acres of ground. Settlers had to learn about new crops. The agricultural objective of giving the settlers a good cash income had to be achieved as soon as possible, because government did not want the settlers to be on rations for too long. But it was going to take five to seven years for the tree crops to produce income-earning crops. And before the planting could take place, heavy stands of tropical rain forest had to be cleared. Never having cleared such large trees before, the Gilbertese found tree felling difficult. So did onlookers—the settler's felling accuracy was at first in the 360-degree range.

The Medical officer, a doctor who had trained in London, had the habit of looking in his books and then declaring that nursing mothers needed this vitamin or that food supplement intake. He knew next to nothing about the value of indigenous foods, such as shellfish and coconut, and wild vegetables from the forest. At the doctor's urging, we arranged for a daily catch of fish. The Gilbertese, trolling for and netting fish, using motorboats supplied by government, collected around 2,000 pounds a day. They were fond of dried shark, whose liver was particularly nutritious.

Tabea, who had been a mechanic on Ocean Island, was a very inventive man. Early on in the resettlement, when I expressed to Tabea my concern that the settlers might spread diseases if they all used the same well, he explained how the Gilbertese had avoided the spread of sickness with their own wells in the Gilberts. He and his friends designed and built several wells with cement walls and railings to prevent animals from getting too close to the water.

Each day, I visited my Gilbertese friends in the three newly constructed resettlement communities: Tekinaiti Tokatake, a former marine officer; and Tabea, an old man who was anxious to help me improve my use of Gilbertese. He wanted me to speak to the people in Gilbertese instead of relying on an interpreter. I progressed and, with help from my anthropologist friend Bill Stuart, was able to translate the Queen's birthday message for 1964 into Gilbertese for an assembled crowd.

Reading

Cochrane, Glynn. 1970a. The Administration of Wagina Resettlement Scheme. Human Organization 29(2):123–132.

___. 1970b. Big Men and Cargo Cults. Oxford: The Clarendon Press.

___. 1971. The Case for Fieldwork by Officials. Man 6(2):279–284.

Firth, Raymond. 1963. We the Tikopia. Boston: Beacon Press.

Hogbin, Ian. 1944. Native Councils and Native Courts in the Solomon Islands. Oceania11(4):257–283.

___. 1958. Social Change. London: Watts.

Marcus, George. 1995. Ethnography in/of the World System: The Emergence of Multi-Sited Ethnography. Annual Review of Anthropology 24:95–117.

Masefield, G. B. 1950. A Short History of Agriculture in the British Colonies. Oxford: Oxford University Press.

White, Geoffrey M. 2003. Identity through History: Living Stories in a Solomon Island Society. New York: Cambridge University Press.

4

℘℘

Festival Elephant Culture Shock in Papua New Guinea and Polynesia

When the first Europeans, gold explorers from Australia, reached the New Guinea highlands in the 1930s, the local people thought they were gods. After the Europeans made sexual advances to local women, the highlanders decided they were not. History proved them right.

When Papua New Guinea achieved its independence from Australia in 1975, its economy consisted of three sectors: traditional horticulture, on which the majority of the Papua New Guinean population still relied for its livelihood; a growing monetized sector, mainly owned or controlled by expatriates, based on plantation agriculture, forestry, small-scale manufacturing, trading, and other service sectors and government operations; and a huge mining enclave project whose effect on the overall employment and income of the Papua New Guinea economy was small. The money economy had been driven by private sector growth—tea, coffee, timber, and mining, which had benefited large companies and entrepreneurs.

Officials in the global aid agencies were blinded by their view that "traditional society" constrained development, that it was an obstacle that needed to be changed as soon as possible. "Culture" was a matter of exotic postcards. Visiting staff who knew nothing of the country and its cultural heritage mailed postcards to the offices back home showing bare-breasted women dancing, highland men in full regalia (feathers and paint known as *bilas*), or women suckling pigs.

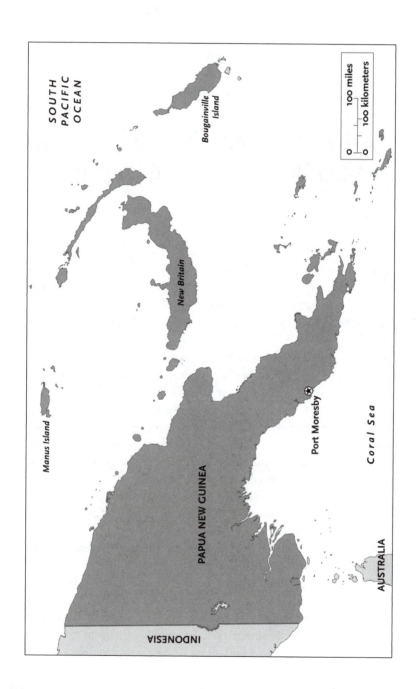

Aid agency advice to Papua New Guinea goes back to 1963, when the World Bank advised the Australian colonial administration to abandon the highlands and concentrate on developing coastal areas. Expatriates, who held much of the flat land on the coast, would be the primary beneficiaries. The adoption of industrialized country forms of productive organization, especially ownership and control of land and farming operations, was considered indispensable for modernizing the rural economy. This approach also meant imposing alien corporate business organization on most of the larger operations, and individual ownership and control of small farms and businesses, rather than working with and adapting traditional communal and clan ownership patterns.

If one could compare the quality of life now in PNG to that of a baseline study conducted in Papua New Guinea in the 1930s, it would show that life has not improved for most people since then—neither by the arrival of outsider entrepreneurs nor by global aid agencies with all the millions of dollars that they have poured into Port Moresby, the capital.

Global development plans failed to take into account variations in local social organization, including differences in men's and women's status. In contexts where women were the leaders and controlled the major resources, their male-biased plans either fell flat by missing the relevant target population or they succeeded in bringing about the decline of women's status.

Father Bruns, a Catholic priest from the Netherlands who had been in Papua New Guinea for fifty years, told Diana Bisena that the people her agency was working with were matriarchal. Diana was from Jakarta and had a doctorate in development sociology from the University of Leiden. She had to look up that word!

Diana considered the possibility that the development teams were missing something of central importance. Most of the projects focused on men, perhaps because her agency was quite patriarchal. She realized, though, that the focus should be on women. They were the ones with the power and tradition. If the agency wanted to help the people, they needed to work through the women. Change the women and they would change the men.

The Father said that he was always telling the women to unite. That way they would be able to control their men. According to Father Bruns, outside aid had mostly hurt the people, not helped them. He said they were developing a "sit around and wait for handouts" thinking and this was destroying their morale and sense of personal value. Agencies should stop thinking money and start thinking people. Programs should be aimed at what is familiar and liked by the people, even if it does not appear to have long-term practical value. He said that traditionally the people needed nothing; it was all there in the jungle. So they had no motivation to learn new or unfamiliar skills. Agencies should build the relationships first and slowly offer new ideas. The people would change, but it would take generations, not one lifetime. He said that Diana's aid agency should continue their emphasis on health and education because that's what matters. They can save only a few, but maybe those few will save their people.

Missing Big Men and Local Leadership Styles

Papua New Guinea, as in much of Melanesia (the region in the South Pacific that stretches from the western part of what is now Indonesia through Papua New Guinea and the Solomon Islands and on to Vanuatu), is characterized by a particular form of local leadership called the "Big Man" system. In it, men (and sometimes, in such places as Vanuatu, women) build political support across several villages through personal charisma and public generosity. They exhort their followers to produce more pigs or yams and contribute surpluses to them periodically that are then the basis of grand feasts at which the followers receive in return gifts of food, money, and other goods. Big Man politics is a redistributive political system based on face-to-face interaction between leaders and followers and on the careful accounting of contributions and redistribution.

The traditional Melanesian Big Man was an entrepreneur. He was able to initiate, organize, and execute tasks of economic and political importance, and do this in a manner that expressed Melanesian values and precepts. In his relationships with his supporters, he ensured, on an everyday basis and gradually over a long period of time, that people felt obligated to him and also admired him.

A traditional leader's status and position depended on a personal display of skill in the accumulation and distribution of resources. His wealth lay in the number of people that he had obligated to him and the fact that he could, at a time of his choice, call on them to discharge their obligations. He transformed the obligations into cash and then spent the cash on feasts and purchases that gave him high status.

The international aid officials were oblivious to these critical features of Papua New Guinean investment. They kept coming up with ideas for development projects, which they then tried to get local leaders to adopt and carry out. Leaders and would-be leaders were not interested in implementing someone else's idea, much less one that did not fit with their aspirations. In traditional society, it was important for a leader to develop his own idea in secret, to which he then dedicated much planning in order to realize it.

Festival Elephants in Papua New Guinea

The Festival Elephants from global aid agencies who arrived in Papua New Guinea in the 1980s were mainly interested in expanding the money economy. The aid officials and the Papua New Guineans did not get to know each other, and so neither understood each other. Nor did the aid officials understand the local ecology and what worked in it. In the 1970s, while flying in a helicopter over the interior highlands of Papua New Guinea, a senior World Bank official noticed extensive grasslands. On returning to his home office, he wrote a memo to his staff proclaiming that his agency's global livestock program should do well in the area. He and his staff generated statistics showing that cattle and pig herds would be a winning investment. The Papua New Guinea government, not wishing to offend such an eminent official, politely accepted a "non-performing" loan in the agricultural sector.

"Non-performing" meant that, even though the loan did not produce what was expected, the Papua New Guinea government still owed the money to the World Bank.

The project soon failed. The highlanders didn't like or understand wire fencing. They were terrified of the cattle and stalked them with rifles and axes. The pigs, a breed known in Denmark for its ability to provide lean bacon, were not popular among local people because they preferred fatty meat. And the pigs suffered from sunburn.

The growing number of failed projects showed that the Myth of Global Poverty hindered the aid agency's ability to deliver development assistance, let alone assistance that reached the very poorest people. Festival Elephants played a major role in the failure of projects in agriculture, health, and education. For example, an integrated rural development project in the highlands proved to be an expensive and overly complicated failure; an agricultural support services project for the entire country had to be cancelled; an oil palm project on Cape Hoskins, on the north coast of New Britain, generated incomes of several thousand dollars for the lucky participants. Those living nearby who were not project participants, however, had incomes of less than US$100 a year. What the developers did succeed in was creating social inequality.

Meanwhile, transportation projects, such as the construction of the Highlands Highway leading up into the central highlands, seemed to do better. At least the road was built and used. Projects that could be engineered and brought to completion by expatriate technical personnel, such as road or bridge projects, were more successful than projects that called for changed behavior on the part of participants.

Misunderstanding Poverty in Papua New Guinea

Only a third of the people in Papua New Guinea in the 1980s used money. In this context, an income-based definition of poverty made little sense. Nevertheless, the global aid officials proceeded to follow the blinding mandate of the Myth of Global Poverty. They carried out statistical analyses in their home offices to measure poverty in Papua New Guinea according to global indicators. Whether their poverty measures or statistical findings were meaningful was never effectively proved. Global assumptions about poverty made as little sense in Papua New Guinea as they did anywhere else.

The aid agency approach to defining what they called *absolute poverty*, and who lived above the absolute poverty line and who lived below it, was to estimate the cost in each region of a certain bundle of goods, or basic needs, required to keep a person or family alive and generally healthy in relation to their energy requirements. Basic needs included mainly costs for food and shelter. While this economic approach might work in monetized contexts such as Chicago or Biarritz, in non-monetized contexts it missed the mark entirely. When there is no shop, how does one measure the costs of food? How was one to know who was eating small jungle animals called *cuscus*, or crocodile?

To measure food energy requirements, the aid officials made an assumption about food energy levels that could maintain the body's metabolic rate at rest. Once the energy intake was determined, and its cost calculated, an allowance for non-food spending could be added by finding the total expenditure level at which a person typically crossed over the poverty line. In the highlands of Papua New Guinea, however, a man might work hard at clearing a garden for several days, and then he might sit and think for a day or two. He might go to war at the weekend with his neighbors or go walkabout, covering long distances and traversing mountain ranges. How could a global formula of dietary needs per capita per year capture such local patterns in any realistic way?

Relationships Between Officials and Local People

In the 1980s, the World Bank staff working on Papua New Guinea's development was based in Washington, D.C. During their two- to three-year assignment, they visited Papua New Guinea three or four times a year for two to three weeks at a time. While in the country, they spent most of their time in the capital city, moving between the Department of Finance and their hotel. A World Bank office was established only in 1989. Prior to their arrival in the country, they had received no special training that would have alerted them to important cultural features of Papua New Guinea, nor were they given any instruction in Pidgin English, which is now the lingua franca, called Tok Pisin.

I took my orders from the Minister for Public Service in Papua New Guinea and his successors who were all outstanding leaders. As a civil servant in the Solomon Islands, I learned that it was my job to work for politicians. In Papua New Guinea, however, I found that aid agency personnel paid little attention to what politicians wanted to do; their general attitude was that the highest duty of a politician was to follow their advice. Although UN officials such as those in the World Bank talked as if they were an International Civil Service, they were, unlike ordinary civil servants, servants without masters. At the World Bank, for example, a Vice President in charge of a region such as Africa considered himself above a Prime Minister, a Director considered himself above a minister, and a Division Chief thought himself superior to the Head of a Government Department.

Aid agency personnel paid little attention to what elected politicians wanted to do. With the aid officials and the technocrats effectively sidelining local politicians, the country was deprived of the contribution of indigenous leaders who were the only people capable of encouraging substantial change at village level.

I was amazed by the way senior Papua New Guinea public servants kept in touch with their home villages. Paul Songo, Chairman of the Public Service Commission, had me to dinner at his house on Touaguba hill and cooked fish he had caught in the sea at Ella Beach, Port Moresby. He came from Manus Island, the smallest of the Provinces, and he liked nothing better than to go home to his village. John Vulupindi, the Secretary for Finance, who came from New Britain, lit up when he talked about home. There was a time of the year—sometime around March—when, he said, if you stood on the edge of the reef, the fish came in to you. I went to New Britain one March and saw, twenty or thirty feet down in the cobalt blue translucent water, fish moving toward the reef. Suddenly one of the fish doubled with a spear through its middle. Deep below the surface a tadpole-like figure with a large belly and little legs moved to the fish and began to shoot to the surface. The fishing apparatus was made from a piece of steel reinforcing rod and two pieces of inner tube rubber, which had been made into a spear gun. The fish was a wonderful, shimmering, luminous yellow and green.

Referring to negotiations with the Australian Government, important because Australia supplied about 40 percent of the Papua New Guinea budget, the Secretary of the Prime Minister's Department complained that "We meet overseas counterparts from Australia and shake hands. Then we move back from the table and our expatriate staff take over. This must stop." It didn't. This collaboration often resulted in politicians being given project papers to read and approve days before the documents were due to be presented for decision in Parliament. Papua New Guinea politicians did not have specialist staff to help them to prepare their own ideas.

This situation arose because the World Bank, in order to push more loans, persuaded the Papua New Guinea government to hire expatriates to serve in key ministries, such as Finance and Planning. These expatriates became an aid agency "fifth column." Throughout the 1970s and 1980s, one could pick up a copy of *The Economist* and see Papua New Guinea advertising for economists and policy analysts. The expatriates, many of whom aspired to a career with a global aid agency, gave priority to advancing the views and projects of the aid agencies. They said openly that they made all the important decisions in the country. They helped put in place global programs and projects by processing the papers for loans. Many of these expatriates in fact did go on to jobs with global aid agencies. One Secretary for Finance joked that he should charge the aid agencies a training fee because so many of the expatriates he had employed ended up with them.

A Cargo Cult Partnership?

Given their relationships with visiting aid officials, Papua New Guinea's senior officials developed a cynical view of the global aid organizations and called visiting aid agency officials "loan salesmen." They were right. At the annual meetings of the World Bank and International Monetary Fund, the Regional Vice President was not shy about saying that Papua New Guinea needed to borrow more money from the World Bank. The agencies promoted their own big picture advice, which prompted more borrowing by PNG. To even up the partnership, the Papua New Guinea officials who interacted with people from the World Bank translated the relationship into their own terms, in much the same way that cult members had thought about cargo in the Solomon Islands: if you performed the right ritual, the cargo would come. Following this logic, in the early 1990s the Papua New Guinea Department of Finance decided to hire one of the World Bank staff in order to learn how to get more money from the Bank. When they employed the Bank's country economist while he was still working on Papua New Guinea, the alarm in Washington, D.C. was similar to that seen when some unworthy country announces that it has acquired nuclear devices. The economist, who was paid several million dollars on a tax-free basis by the Papua New Guinea government, had worked on national income, the exchange rate, consumption, savings, investment, profits, imports, exports, rates of population growth, and debt management. As a World Bank "country economist," he was responsible each year for writing an economic memorandum dealing with Papua New Guinea's creditworthiness, and then defining the World Bank's strategy for the next few years. So he was in a position to know what the World Bank thought of the government's economic policies and performance, and what they intended to do to improve matters. He also knew what other donors, such as the European Union and Australia, thought were the top priorities.

Yeunis Khan, a consultant economist, worked for global aid agencies to help them build models of the economy in client countries. Yeunis was born in Lahore, Pakistan, and educated in Europe and the United States. In his doctoral dissertation, which was about the US chemical industry, he demonstrated the value of risk analysis based on strict quantitative methods. Yeunis believed that every obstacle one met in life could be overcome with the application of disciplined economic logic.

While on a professional visit to the Philippines he discovered that the elevator in his office's building, the best building in Manilla, often stopped between floors. As a result, he had been late for his squash game. In the future, he would use the stairs when he left work in the afternoon, thus guarding against a personal time cost. In the morning, on the way to his office, he took the elevator because, if it stopped, the agency would bear the cost.

The economy, to Yeunis, was not an intellectual abstraction but a reality with physical and chemical properties whose changes and states he incorporated into his everyday language. There was heating up and cooling down, expansion and contraction, liquidity and rigidity, adjustment and equilibrium. The economy was also a contraption; it had levers and balances, upswings and downswings, surges, shocks, and elasticity. The economy was a global phenomenon: it was, like the laws of physics, not subject to local cultural rules or variations.

Public Service Reform

From 1975 until 1985, the size of the public service in Papua New Guinea doubled from 26,000 to 52,000 employees. Discipline was lax, with only eighty disciplinary proceedings a year. Thirty-five percent of all employees did not have the minimum qualifications for their job. In 1980, the 50,000-strong civil service in Papua New Guinea had the same organizational structures to run the public service with 2,000 expatriates as it had with 19,000 expatriates in the public service prior to independence. It took up to two years to hire an expatriate.

Prior to the country's independence, local administrative capacity was underdeveloped because policy decisions and administrative control for Papua New Guinea remained centralized in Canberra, Australia, as late as 1968. The Australian Administrator in Port Moresby was merely a coordinator without the prestige and authority of a British colonial Governor. Within PNG the Administration did not delegate major responsibilities to the district and the local levels. The PNG public service was without significant local participation, and thus de facto was an extension of the Australian public service, dominated by Australian values and methods. Academic observers in the 1970s felt that the Australian administrative system, combined with its centralization in Canberra and Port Moresby, was overcomplicated and too costly for the needs of the country.

In 1983, and at the request of the Government of Papua New Guinea and the World Bank, I took leave from my university position in the United States and went to Port Moresby as World Bank Public Administration Advisor to assist with a project on Public Sector Reform. I spent four years assisting the PNG government to create a more effective and responsive public service. In order to achieve this goal, the constitutionally entrenched position of the Public Service Commission (PSC) had to be altered. The PSC had enjoyed the right to create employment and to make pay awards without the approval of the executive branch; it also handled discipline and training.

After four years, the minister for public services in PNG managed to get a constitutional amendment that I had drafted passed by parliament—it required three separate approvals in three separate parliamentary sittings. The amendment changed the role and function of the Public Service Commission to permit the government to have more say in the management of public service. It turned the Public Service Commission from an executive authority into an advisory body. The amendment passed by 109 votes to 4 abstentions.

I then worked with officers in the Finance and Public Service departments to produce a new Public Service Management Act and a new Public Finance Management Act. These pieces of legislation gave elected politicians much more say about how the Public Service operated while, we hoped, guarding against undue politicization. The Public Finance Act has been used on several occasions to prosecute instances of corruption.

Once the enabling legislation was passed, it became possible to turn to performance improvement. This part of the reform began with the central agencies—the ones whose legislation had been changed, plus the National Planning Office and the Prime Minister's Department. Task Forces were established. They examined how the central agencies were organized, the policy framework, the staffing, and the budgetary resources in order to draw up action proposals for the chief executive in each of these departments. Following that exercise, reform was extended to cover line departments in important revenue-generating ministries such as agriculture as well as minerals and energy. The next task was to look at the departments responsible for service delivery. These resource management reviews of the central agencies of government, conducted by the Management Development Unit that I had established with UNDP/World Bank assistance, sought and obtained the views of clients at all levels.

Civil Service Reform Informed by Local Culture

Papua New Guinea people who worked in the public service were responsive to their village ties and to local rules about social responsibility and exchange. For example, the secretary of a department might give more weight to the views of the local man who served him tea because the tea server was from the secretary's home village. Village values were important, and senior PNG public servants maintained close ties with their home village.

I hoped that reorganization of the public service in Papua New Guinea would follow the Melanesian principles that I knew from my time in the Solomon Islands. I did not agree with the writings of the German sociologist, Max Weber, who thought that a public service bureaucracy was separated from society. To my mind, the public service in Papua New Guinea was simply another form of social organization, and it should reflect the local cultural values and beliefs. Oratory was important in traditional PNG society, and so it was likely that verbal communication skills would be much more important than writing ability. A Melanesian civil service would not need the masses of rules and regulations left behind by the Australians that covered such exotica as an allowance for owners of aircraft and the lengthy bureaucratic procedures that an officer could invoke if he wished to decline promotion.

It seemed sensible to design a public service with the same minimal hierarchy as that found in the villages where there were only Big Men who were the leaders and other people who were not. The Australians, in order to serve Papua New Guinea society, had created a public service with eleven categories of clerk (the Australian term for all ranks of public servant). At the top was the secretary. He usually had a single deputy, although in the Agriculture and Prime Minister's Departments there were two deputy secretaries. Under the deputy was one to three, or even four, First Assistant Secretaries. Under them were Assistant Secretaries. Under the Assistant Secretaries was a hierarchy of clerks beginning with a clerk who might well be a graduate, down to a Class 1 or Class 2 clerk who was unskilled.

A civil service needs to be able to move talent quickly up through the ranks. One of the strengths of traditional Papua New Guinea society was the fact that fresh leadership was continually coming forward because ambitious young men were continually trying to become Big Men. So it was important to find ways of not tying up the top spots in the public service. The institution of short-term contracts for department secretaries facilitated turnover at the top. Leadership had another very important function because, in traditional society, discipline was imposed by Big Men and the ready acceptance of that discipline by village people was an obvious strength for development activities. There were gaps to be filled. Women had not yet reached the most senior levels of the public service, but because attitudes in the village were beginning to shift, it was reasonable to expect that an increasing number of women would get top jobs.

The public service was not just one social organization—hardly likely in a country with seven hundred language groups. Managers in the public service were always tempted to yield to social pressure by trying to help kinsmen or friends from their home area, people known as Wan Toks ("One Talks"), or those who spoke the same language as they did. The best way to ensure that merit played a proper role was to reinforce the objectivity and integrity of the system for appointments, promotions, and terminations.

Local Government Reforms

The local government arrangements established during the Australian colonial era were awarded low priority by aid agencies. Visiting aid officials had little interest in field administration and no frequent contact with provincial officials. Communication would have been difficult in remote areas because the aid officials did not learn Pidgin English and so could not talk to people in the provinces. Aid agencies did encourage the government to preserve and strengthen the hands-on patrol system created by the Australians, something that would have helped poor people. In a subsistence economy with widely dispersed populations and difficult terrain, it was essential to have staff spending time in the villages in order to monitor people's welfare. A great strength of the Australian period was the establishment of a system of regular patrolling in even the most remote areas.

This patrol system was similar to the touring system that the British had used in the Solomons. Each district in the country had a resident district commissioner, district officers, and patrol officers who spent much of their time in the bush visiting remote villages. Young patrol officers went from village to village on a regular basis, bringing not only law and order with them but also medical and educational supplies.

Some years after independence was granted in 1975, the Papua New Guinea government introduced a system of provincial government, a system whose boundaries were the same as the old districts in the colonial era. This reform was a result of pressure from the island of Bougainville, which wanted independence from PNG. National politicians viewed the new creation as a political animal that had been set up to give vent to regional aspirations with the hope that secessionist tendencies such as those on Bougainville would be alleviated. A system of grants from central government was introduced, which, while providing some funds, did not allow the new authorities to live in quite the grand manner to which they aspired. To get extra money, the provinces had to apply for grants and loans, which meant that they had to have competent staff. The larger provinces had the money to hire the staff they needed, but the smaller provinces did not. So, one result of the new local government system was an increase in inequality. Rich provinces became richer and poor provinces became poorer.

Over time, provincial capitals became like miniature versions of Port Moresby. Provincial staff sat in their offices and waited for clients to call. They did not travel throughout the region in order to keep in touch with local problems. With help from the Department of Finance, we were able to put in place a UNDP World Bank-executed project to help strengthen provincial government. Four provinces were chosen in which to initiate the project: North Solomons, Southern Highlands, Manus, and East Sepik. Over the course of the next two years, teams from the Program Management Unit visited each of these provinces repeating at the provincial level the exercise we had just undertaken at the national level.

Festival Elephants Performing in the Cook Islands

In 1990, I took a UNDP-funded job as Public Administration Advisor for the Prime Minister of the Cook Islands, Sir Geoffrey Henry. I was to look after civil service reform. In the Cook Islands, the number of civil servants had been growing at an unsustainable rate, and if these trends continued, the government would not be able to afford to provide them with the resources to do their jobs. Part of the problem was that the civil service was really the only available job in the outer islands, and all those employed could be counted on to support the politician who had hired them. A second concern was to ensure that ministers were able to have some say in the appointment and service of the heads of departments they had to work with. In other words, politicians did not want to run the civil service, but they did want to have civil servants who they could work with on a day-to-day basis.

Building on my Papua New Guinea experience, I helped to draft legislation on changing the role and function of the Public Service Commission. My goal was to ensure that the Commission, while safeguarding the integrity of the civil service, did not continue to hire people as if money was not a problem.

The Cook Islands were host to many visiting UN officials, all of whom were interested in pushing their organization's agenda, wanting the Cooks to support this or that initiative or take on this or that project or program. Sir Geoffrey Henry once held up a clock at a UN conference in New York and said, "You see the time on this clock is New York time, not Cook Islands time."

Today's aid agencies are not the first developers who discovered that things did not turn out as expected. Following the arrival of missionaries in the Cooks, traditional taboos against sexual inter-course for one or two years following childbirth broke down, and peo-ple no longer used abortifacients (substances that induce abortion) or infanticide as indigenous means of family planning. Missionaries and Europeans have, since their first arrival, been known as *papa'aa*. This means "seven layers of clothing" and refers to the fact that when the local men turned the women missionaries upside down to see what they were like, they discovered that they had, with all their petticoats, seven layers of clothing. The missionary "improvements" had unin-tended consequences. Better public health lowered infant mortality. The outlawing of infanticide and euthanasia increased life expectancy. The overall result: population densities on many of the small islands are now as high as in cities in industrialized countries. The introduc-tion of cash-cropping for export used up the best garden-land on many islands, so that land that was previously dedicated to growing food for home consumption was no longer available.

The Cook Islands

The Cook Islands are a group of 15 small islands scattered over 1,360,000 kilometers of the Pacific Ocean. Their land area is only 234 kilometers. The northern islands, Manihiki, Nassau, Penrhyn (also called Tongureva or Mangarongaro), Pukapuka, Rakahanga, and Suwarrow are atolls. Of the southern group, Aitutaki, Atiu, Man-gaia, Mauke, Mitiaro, and Rarotonga are volcanic islands, while Palmerston, Manuae, and Takutea are uninhabited atolls.

The Cook Islands have been inhabited for about 1,000 years. In terms of contact with Europeans, Álvaro de Mendaña de Neira in 1595 was the first to arrive; he came from Spain by way of Peru. In 1775, Captain James Cook, after whom the islands are named, arrived. His name has lasted far longer than Captain Cook did.

Cook Islanders today still know the sea, and they are mighty voy-agers in their great canoes or *vakas*. In 1356, some Cook Islanders left their crowded home and went to seek a better life in the then-uninhab-ited New Zealand. They still make voyages to New Zealand or to Hawai'i for fun, and to show that they still can do it. Voyaging is the Cook Islanders' response to poverty or a downturn in the economy.

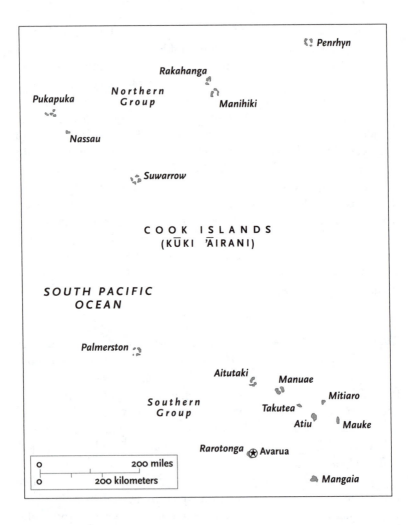

All Cook Islanders are citizens of New Zealand, so they can come and go as they please. Most have a place in the Cook Islands and relatives in New Zealand.

The Cook Islands were colonized by New Zealand, and from 1901 to 1965 they were a New Zealand territory. Since then, they have been self-governing but with a very close association with New

Zealand. They depend on New Zealand for defense and external relations.

The economy is based on agricultural exports, tourism, exports of cultured pearls, the sale of offshore fishing, and an extremely enterprising offshore banking industry. The Cook Islands developed a thriving offshore banking industry that rivaled the Cayman Islands in the Caribbean. Alan Bond, the Australian financier, regularly passed money through the Cook's offshore banking industry. For domestic banking, Cook Islanders like to have at least one member of the family who has a job in the government. Most of those who work in the government also have interests in farming and tourism. They produce wonderful pork because the pigs are fed papaya and coconuts. The tourism industry has expanded enough so that most men and women can get a full- or part-time job in a hotel or guesthouse.

An aid agency engineer approached the government about the possibility of mining manganese. The deposit lay on the seabed within the country's territorial waters. He had been given photographs of manganese nodules sitting, like so many billiard balls, on the floor of the South Pacific Ocean, and, he was told, worth billions of dollars. He had developed, and wanted to arrange, funding for a never-previously used idea for retrieving the manganese. As he gave details of how he intended to attract private sector investors, the audience began to look pleased. Indeed, at one point in his animated presentation, one of the islanders said to another, "If he can suck as well as he can blow he'll have no trouble getting the nodules up."

The population of the Cook Islands in 2007 was about 18,000. Over half live on Rarotonga, the largest island as well as the business and administrative center. They, like other Polynesians, have a political system based on hereditary status with kings and queens. The leadership, called Ariki, has ritual functions in the traditional belief system. Some leaders still have distributive functions with respect to land or access to economic opportunities. They are a symbol for the people: to be, to eat, and to live well and, by so doing, to provide a sense of prosperity for followers.

Aid Agency Initiatives

Workshops that aim to improve the diet of the Cook Islanders by teaching them to grow and eat green vegetables and citrus fruits continue to be very popular. But the question of what can be grown is of course different from what will be grown. Nutrition experts discover that Cook Islanders are like the Scots: They do not like vegetables. They want scones and jam and sugar, and they have a particular fondness for condensed milk. Unsuccessful attempts to improve nutrition have a long history. A hundred years previously, visiting missionaries left a sow and a boar as breeding stock on a small Pacific island hoping that this gift would turn the inhabitants away from the consumption of human flesh. The islanders proceeded to worship the pigs and fed them their best-cooked taro. The first litter was sacrificed to the gods as a mark of respect.

Cook Islanders have an excellent sense of humor. When the islanders heard I was an anthropologist, they said they knew I would be interested in kinship, and so told me a story about the Finance Minister's wife who liked to go to the movies; the Finance Minister didn't. One night the projector broke, the wife returned to find him in bed with his mother-in-law, who was supposed to be minding the kids. The mother-in-law became pregnant. His brothers and sisters called the child that was born, "the Finance Minister's son." He was his sister's stepson, and he was also his nephew, and his niece's "uncle."

The islanders have been studied by many university researchers seeking their place in the sun, or a share of someone's budget. Researchers run workshops and seminars on migration, celestial navigation, mythology, architecture, cooking, child-rearing, tying string figures, making tapa cloth, fire-walking, remittances from overseas, and so on. Thirty years ago, the South Pacific Commission in Noumea looked at a wide range of subjects that were of importance for island life and so did the Musée de l'homme in Paris. The South Pacific Commission in Noumea produced a whole series of "Atoll Research Bulletins."

Traditional Political Organization

During the New Zealand colonial era, the important position of the traditional Polynesian leaders in the Cooks, known as Ariki, was weakened, which dealt a body blow to local society from which the society has never recovered. Neither missionaries nor politicians have been able to replace the role of the Ariki as the lynchpin of Cook Island society. The traditional Ariki were stern taskmasters. They got their people to work, and persuaded their people to invest in the future. In traditional times, Ariki held their jobs so long as they behaved well. They could be dismissed for incompetence. Since the colonial era and their loss of status, no Ariki has been dismissed for incompetence.

In the Cook Islands, as elsewhere in Polynesia, distribution of material goods rather than the creation or accumulation of wealth is important. He or she who would be an Ariki distributes goods. The very act of public giving confirms status. Global aid projects in the Cook Islands made it possible for well-off politicians, who were often of chiefly birth, to act like Ariki. Thus they increased the status and wealth of those who already had it. In giving out the jobs and the equipment associated with projects, the Ariki looked after their friends and relatives. The public expectation was, and it is a socially sanctioned expectation, that those at the top must do so. A local member of the Cook Islands Parliament who brought aid money to the islands would gain considerable status, regardless of whether or not the projects worked. Local people assumed that aid was a matter of distribution, a matter of picking the right men in Parliament to have as a friend. Thus, they reshaped global aid into their local cultural system of redistribution and sharing.

The big problem for poor islanders is not low income or some other deficient quality of life statistic; it is the absence of family members through migration, premature death from illness or accidents at sea. Poverty as it is defined in the Cooks is not something that the government can do much to alleviate, so poor Cook Islanders did not look to their government or to aid agencies for much help.

The wealth of the area is not its beauty or the strength of its people; it is the strength of the community. The local community is solid. It has strong religious beliefs, low rates of crime or deviance, and a limited ambition to join the outside world. In such small communities, change has very local implications; acceptance or rejection depends on local perception, history, personalities, epidemics, and cyclones.

෨෨

Now, what to do this morning in Rarotonga? Yesterday, Etienne Debernay, a French economist who worked for a global aid agency headquartered in New York City, had felt in a sportive mood. He had gone on a
fishing boat with a group of young people who drank huge amounts of
sweet rum. He was immediately struck by one young couple: they were
both thin and tall, pasty white with a patchwork of angry little red bites on
their legs. Their eyes were glassy, and their lips looked squashed, as if
they were always kissing an invisible pane of glass. They self-consciously
chose not to sit with each other, though they took care not to be far apart.
Both had headphones on and both were listening to some sort of music
coming from a small stereo box placed between them. They must have
gone to university. He wondered if they had read any of his work. He was,
after all, a well-known economist.

In Etienne Debernay's life, there was not enough soil for anything
female to take root. He couldn't tolerate a woman who did nothing,
wrote nothing, and said nothing. If they worked, then they were com-
petitors, and so he couldn't stand them either. To be sure, he felt the
same way about men. He needed much more space than was possible
if there were people all around, always needing something or disturb-
ing you.

The French social scientist Emile Durkheim had explained his concept of *anomie* as a state of uneasiness or painful anxiety occasioned by
the fact that despite doing one's best to do what society wanted, one
failed to experience happiness. Blinking into the sun, Etienne thought
it useful to start with this idea since it was true. The situation was
anomic. Now he must come up with something creative for the poor of
the world. The feelings that one had about one's own creative intellect
were not easy to communicate. From the point of view of that intellect's needs, social life might be carried on in what appeared to be a
normal fashion, but it didn't really have meaning and substance. Having this creative intellect was like possessing an incredibly good piece
of machinery. It had awesome power and could solve problems with
contemptuous ease.

The sun was already hot on the island when Etienne, while walking through the garden, saw a small mouse in the swimming pool. It seemed older and more elongated than the several young ones that had already been recovered from the bottom of the pool on previous mornings. It would have been interesting to know how long it had been there, tail down, pink nose in the air, graying hair, engaged in the utterly impossible task of trying to survive; impossible, that was, without help. Seizing a net, Etienne rescued the mouse, putting it in the sun and watching anxiously until it limped off. Ah, he thought, a safety net for a Third World mouse. The satisfaction the rescuer felt stemmed from a sense of kinship with the mouse—they both had red noses and a large measure of determination when dealing with life's adversities.

There the analogy ended and Etienne could not extract further useful meaning from the incident. Instead, he resumed his morose contemplation of the picture postcard view from the hotel on the side of a hill opposite. In another few days, the conference would be over and he would have to go back to the awful winter in the U.S. Merde, he thought, and had another pastis.

Since coming down to the island with a few colleagues to develop a new approach to sparking growth in the Cook Islands, Etienne had become accustomed to having a gin and tonic early in the morning. He and his colleagues worked alone in the morning and met in the afternoon. In the evening, he usually tried not to have to go out with the others. They were such boring people, so crude, so uninformed. He nodded and murmured to the waiter. Murmuring was something waiters the world over seemed to understand. They always knew if you were the kind of person who could murmur.

Etienne stretched his long legs and eased his thin frame into the deep cushions of a cane chair on the polished wood floor of the veranda. Grateful for the cool breeze, he tucked his brightly colored cravat into his white silk shirt. Etienne took off his rimless glasses and gazed with muted priapic enthusiasm through a large telescope at the young things in various states of undress on the white sand of a nearby island.

Global Projects in Local Places: A Festival Elephant Cautionary Tale

In 1991, I went with some aid agency officials to the Northern Group to inspect donor projects. Everything in the Northern Group is below the national average: education is weak, the diet is inadequate, money-making opportunities don't exist, and freedom of expression is constrained by kinship ties. Islanders do not seem interested in preserving the environment. They eat any rare birds they can trap, overfish the lagoons, dump rubbish in the lagoons, leave old refrigerators lying around, and heave old batteries into streams. They do not have much interest in progressive projects such as exploiting solar energy potential, trying hydroponic gardening, or "mainstreaming" women into development.

Part of my remit as Advisor to the Prime Minister was to see that more aid resources went to strengthening development in the Outer Islands government. The main island, Rarotonga (located in the Southern Group), got a major share of resources and budgetary allocations. In effect, Rarotonga was the central government and the Outer Islands, as they were called, was local government.

During my time, the small UNDP team that was helping me managed to build a consensus that the Outer Islands needed more attention. We also managed to establish administrative arrangements in Rarotonga to make sure that Outer Island development received a higher priority in government circles. We made a determined effort to allocate more skilled professionals to the Outer Islands and to build up a pipeline of locally appropriate and culturally sound development projects. There was agricultural potential—crops such as papaya and vanilla, for example—but building up an export market took time and effort because not only had contacts to be made with countries such as Japan, but strict quarantine regimes had to be established for quality control, and packaging had to be in place, with some certainty of regular supply established. There was also demand for taro from the Pacific island population living in Los Angeles.

The visit was a testament to the international nature of assistance: New Zealand, Australia, Canada, Germany, Japan, Finland, and the

UN system were variously involved in the projects we visited. For the aid agency officials, it was their first and probably last trip to the Northern Group and perhaps even to the South Pacific. Moreover, they didn't really want to be assigned to the South Pacific. They wanted to work on China or Russia or some other large country, or on a global policy study that would get international exposure.

It was extremely difficult to make a reputation in a global aid agency by working in a small country. Small countries did not get much money, and they did not generate policy headlines. Not much would happen if you rushed into headquarters in New York and said, "Do you know what we managed to do in the Northern Cooks?" Since aid agency staff does not attach much importance to small countries such as the Cook Islands, they relied more and more on consultants to process the project paperwork. The excessive use of international consultants often means that much of the money provided as aid ends up back in the rich countries. Some years ago, USAID estimated that of every aid dollar spent overseas, ninety-four cents ended up back in the U.S. because of equipment purchased in the U.S. and expert salaries paid in the U.S. The Cook Islands would probably not be an exception.

The arrival of more and more Festival Elephants in the global aid agencies has affected the Cook Islands, as it has Papua New Guinea, by producing more projects that have failed and very few projects whose benefits have reached the poor. International donors had developed project documents for the Cooks on the basis of work undertaken by consultant teams who knew little about the islands. In some instances, the voluminous project paperwork was completed by exchange of letters and faxes. In other instances, the visiting consultant teams asked the islanders to answer many survey questions about what they wanted or liked, what they didn't want or like, and what they used to want and like. It is difficult to get high quality information on such short visits; islanders often simply tell the visitors what they think they would want to hear. How could they put themselves in the shoes of locals, in order to work out "now what sort of project would I like to have?" Communication was not improved by the islanders' love of avoiding what Europeans would see as the main point of a meeting or conversation. The islanders, who talked to each other all day long before books and videos had arrived, knew how to spin things out. They also knew that when you live in a small community, you must be very gentle about getting to the point. Getting to the point, so important in the Western view, is downright insensitive in their view.

The donor idea that their projects could improve life for the islanders was mistaken. Reliance on projects is slow and bureaucratic. It takes about two years to put into place the aid-funded equipment and the staff for a project. At the end of the two- or three-year project cycle, the vehicles and equipment are sold at bargain prices to private citizens—usually those in the know—after Boards of Survey. By that time, the aid agency staff has usually passed on to better things, allowing the whole cycle to start again. A new set of visitors with a new set of career needs appears and new documents, which describe the old problems in new ways with new approaches, can then be processed.

The aid visitors who arrived for their visit to the Northern Group were all junior donor officials. They expected to see that their projects had contributed to local well-being. It seemed reasonable for them to suppose that their efforts would have been more successful than those of the colonial New Zealanders who had been called "pooh-bahs" after a character in the Mikado. They looked apprehensively from their small boat in the boiling surf at the slippery, slime-covered steps up to the wharf. Up above, the Boy's Brigade band, ramrod straight, resplendent in uniformed white shirts, brass buckles, and long black trousers, played "It's a Long Long Way to Tipperary," and "Where, Tell Me Where Has My Highland Laddie Gone?" more or less at the same time.

Few of the donor officials in the small boat wanted to make the trip so far north of Rarotonga since there was no hotel on the island. Reluctance to visit regularly was increased by the fact that a round trip to the islands cost over US$500 to fly to the nearest airport. The journey to visit the island council at Rakahanga, a small coral atoll south of the equator, had taken a long time by open boat in a heavy sea. The boatmen, preferring theological to development assistance, prayed in Manihiki for a good twenty minutes before starting the trip, and gave hearty thanks when landfall was made at Rakahanga Island. While at sea the wind kept away the heavy oppressive heat, and the swarms of flies and mosquitoes that infested the island and its 300 inhabitants. While the boat was some distance away from Rakahanga, we sighted a few straggly coconut trees. A sour smile lit up the face of an accompanying local official. He said he had sent so much cement to the island that he feared it might have been entirely concreted over.

Met by the Chief Administrative Officer for the island, the party made its way off the broken wharf and past a small gazebo, in which, with the exercise of very little imagination, one could see an army band playing for a Victorian audience chewing happily on cucumber sandwiches. However, this gazebo had been intended to offer shelter to officials while they awaited the politician's arrival. In the aid documents, it was referred to as a "rest-shelter for laborers," a nice touch. The most useful thing Rakahanga people could think to do with it was to sleep on the cool cement floor when the mosquitoes got too bad in their homes which were situated inland.

The visiting aid officials found that the Islanders did not seem to look directly at them. Contact was made with the eyes; a slight widening of the eyes was a sign of recognition. When they walked, the islanders looked pigeon-toed. Closer inspection would have shown that they placed the whole foot on the ground and spread the weight evenly. People who walk in the rain forest do this, because such a positioning of the feet helps to provide traction on mountainous mud paths. Men who are accustomed to walking on sharp coral reefs learn to do the same thing. But it is always hard for Europeans, who have been brought up to put weight on the balls of the feet, to feel entirely comfortable with those who have more erect posture. This erect posture and the customs of the place do not encourage the close physical contact that some Europeans believe to be a sign of warmth.

The visitors were unlucky to have arrived on a Sunday. No swimming or sports or other recreation was allowed. Alcohol was a complete no-no. Those on the island were supposed to go to church three times a day, where they could enjoy really old-fashioned hell and brimstone sermons. However, the experience of spending Sunday on the island also had a useful side, since it became obvious that the really important people in the Outer Islands were the clergy, not the senior government officials.

Before leaving the capital, Rarotonga, for the Northern Group the visitors had met with the Secretary of Agriculture. He explained to the meeting that the country had not had a new agricultural policy for ten years. The policy document, produced with considerable prodding and help from the donors, was over a hundred pages in draft with many statistical annexes. When it was finished, it would go to the Cook Islands Government where it was unlikely that it would be challenged. The agricultural economist from the UN Food and Agricultural Organization in Rome explained that it was the national economy that concerned them. He had removed all proposals for subsidies of any kind. He had concluded that only a third of the country had a good agricultural future because it could sell to the tourist industry. Yes, he realized that meant the poorer regions would remain poor. But please, he said, be sensible. North and south Italy had this problem; northern Scotland and western Ireland had this problem. It would not get better by wasting money. While it might be true that class-one soils in poor regions could grow commercial crops, transport costs were too high. Those regions could grow animal feed. For the suitable areas, he favored land zoning and price supports. They were going to create the right policy and regulatory market. When the farmers got the right signals, they would produce.

Snorts of disbelief came from a senior Cook Island planner in the Agricultural Department who pointed out that there would be lags, that the market was not perfect; information simply did not reach farmers. What if the animal production side collapsed? What if there were technological advances that made production possible in the poorer areas? The UN Food and Agriculture Organization man was unmoved. He was adamant that the plan would not tell people what to do, nor was the price support just a subsidy: it was income support. They would have to give up the idea of exporting in the poor regions. Domestic opportunities were what had to be pursued.

We made our way through the broken rubble of the roadway linking the village to the wharf, whose construction had been organized by a cousin of the Minister for Fisheries. The road, built by a "blend" of donor finance, had been damaged by a cyclone. It might have fared a little better had less cement been siphoned off for the many fine new cement houses owned by the inhabitants. Of course the fact that there was only one cement mixer on the island, in private hands, and whose owner did not know how to make good cement, had not helped either. On shore, to the left of the road, stood a large copra shed (built for processing copra, or dried coconut meat from which coconut oil is produced). Built seven years earlier, it was designed to contain a large walk-in freezer and visitors' accommodations. A local pastor had come up with the accommodation idea. He wanted students from other islands to visit his parish. The regional idea was helpful, because it enabled more "blending" of donor funds, even if there never was anything regional in the commercial cooperation between the islands. Nobody made copra any more in the Northern Group, since the price had dropped below NZ$500 per ton. Nobody was able to figure out what to do with the building. The freezer had not functioned during the last year because it had no generator. It probably never would be economical to run, because the donors had never correctly calculated the cost of power to run the very large freezer, or the cost of freight to transport fish from Rakahanga Island to Rarotonga. These operating costs were prohibitive, and the use of solar power, which might have provided a cheaper alternative, had not been considered. The upstairs accommodations for visitors had never been completed because supplies had never arrived.

To the right of the road was an unfinished hardball court; it would have been difficult to play on during the day because the sun was so hot. Just beyond the unfinished hardball court was the shed for the generator, which had never arrived, and the shed for the workshop, which had never been finished. A building intended to be a sawmill completed the unfinished complex. The Germans had paid for this. However, there was so much co-mingling of funds that it would have been difficult to say who was responsible.

In the Northern Group, skin diseases were common, due to the poor personal hygiene caused by inadequate water supplies and use. Swarms of flies and mosquitoes posed a constant threat to health. Dengue was present, even though several attempts had been made to reduce the vector population through spraying. Water tanks provided by the Australian government were crumbling and uncovered. The local Council's resources were limited because there was only an annual grant of NZ$3000 and the Council was unwilling to impose any charges on the local people in order to meet the cost of its operations. The Council learned from central government that imposing charges and fees could cost an election.

Across the lagoon was a ruined airfield, destroyed by a cyclone—not surprisingly, because it had been constructed right beside the sea and about at sea level. A better site would have meant the loss of thousands of coconut trees. Something even worse happened on a neighboring island where an airfield was constructed on an old coconut plantation. Instead of digging out the palms, the constructors cut them off at ground level and then added a layer of crushed coral over the whole field. Some years later, after three planes had damaged their landing gear in the holes created by the decaying stumps of the palm trees, the authorities learned it would cost over US$1 million to repair the field.

A fishing project financed by Canada had supplied a boat, with the goal of teaching the people of Penrhyn how to catch commercial quantities of fish, and an onshore freezer so they could store their fish until it could be picked up and sent to market in Australia or New Zealand. The boat stayed for only one year, which didn't seem a realistic period for people to learn a new way of making a living. When the project ended and the fishing boat went away to another island, people returned to fishing as they always had. An expatriate brought good money onto the island for a few years, working the freezer and selling the packaged fish in Rarotonga, but then the council wanted more from him for a license renewal and he left.

With great difficulty, a hospital boat had been purchased by the government for Penrhyn using Australian, New Zealand, and Canadian funds. Equipped with a 240-horsepower motor, it proved an attraction to a visiting politician. He offered to pay for the petrol for a spin round the 9-km lagoon—a short trip, which to his surprise cost almost $250. Some months later the gas-guzzler mysteriously sank at its moorings. The boat had cost around US$70,000. Aid staff responsible for the project eventually realized that the islanders would rather eat tinned mackerel in tomato sauce than fresh tuna.

Although the donor projects inspected by the visitors were located in the Outer Islands as were most of the poorest people, none of the donors were interested in strengthening local government. The Local Council staff and politicians had never had any formal training in doing their jobs. They had never been told what they were supposed to be doing. A new set of Council members came every three years. The old members took their records with them, so the new members started from scratch. The main activities of council and central government were similar. Both wanted to fix and/or control roads, wharves, airfields, water, garbage, and any moneymaking proposals. Councils even wanted the central government to give them the resources to do these things. By day, a tractor did work for the government; by night, with the same driver, it was a Council tractor.

The decline in community discipline and church influence in the 1980s resulted in unsightly and unhealthy rubbish piling up everywhere. Local government didn't have the resources to undertake collections; central government did not seem to have the will to undertake prosecutions. Water catchments were not looked after—tanks crumbled, their covering had been taken for other purposes, and larvicide was not used to kill young mosquitoes at the top of water tanks. Typhoid was diagnosed and, without its own doctor, Rakahanga lost at least one young child from its already small population of children. Local and central government blamed each other for the universally poor and deteriorating state of the roads.

In the Outer Islands, local and central government were joined at the head like two Siamese twins. But the bodies fought with each other. Politics, usually quite unnecessary politicking, supplied the lubrication for this antagonism. On Rakahanga, a so-called democratic council conspired to make the Chief Administrative Officer's (CAO) job extremely difficult. On Manihiki, the Mayor subtly invoked the specter of a central government increasingly desperate to raise funds from the local pearl industry. On Penrhyn, people said that an axis between the Council and the national political body had been formed in order to drive home the idea that northern islands were the preserve of national politicians.

This impression could have been buttressed by reading the rather strange legislation on Outer Island Councils. Members of Parliament had been made ex-officio members. Since the member on Manihiki was also Minister for Marine Resources and in conflict with the mayor, this had potentially interesting implications. How the minister would have dealt with an appeal from a member of the public against a council decision on a marine matter was not clear.

Throughout the Northern Group, the Mayor and the CAO resident on the island were political animals and natural enemies. On Rakahanga, the Democratic Party Mayor spent a good deal of time obstructing or certainly not helping the CAO, who was appointed by the Cook Islands Party which was in power. On Manihiki, the Mayor had co-opted the CAO. On Penrhyn, the Mayor was destined to win shortly, since his number two was going to take over from the CAO.

The Penrhyn Council members gamboled optimistically from visitor to visitor in the hope that aid funds might be provided, which would not only enable them to finish the personal projects they were interested in, but would also avoid even discussion of the need to impose any charges. The politician who was Deputy Minister for Marine Resources wanted to open up the lagoon to pearl fishing. Perhaps for this reason the Mayor had been given a supervisory job with the Public Works Department at almost twice the average salary. The deputy mayor was given the job of Chief Administrative Officer.

The Council was not really a local government body. It was instead a public service association, since all the members were public servants. They were elderly, tired people who belonged to a different political party from the one currently in power. Their politician benefactor also belonged to their party. But the Chief Administrative Officer, the government representative on the island, was a man appointed by the politicians then in power. He and the Council spent a good deal of time trying to confound or confuse each other. This did not really get in the way of government business, because the government had very little business.

And, in any event, the Council wanted to do the same things as the government, except in one respect. The Council wanted to rehabilitate the island's taro swamp, an important source of food, which periodically suffered from incursions of seawater. Their plan involved building, at someone else's expense, huge cement dykes—a task that might have offered an opportunity to finish the remaining cement houses on the island or to finance the construction of new ones. It was a task worthy of a South Pacific pharaoh. The zeal with which the Council members pursued the matter suggested that they had been told that aid officials liked infrastructure projects.

Not much of the public's business was done. Although charged with responsibility for road maintenance, the Council had fallen down on the job. The only employment on the island was provided by public service positions, most of which had been created in order to secure some government or other in office.

The next island to be visited was Manihiki, which had a population of little over 300. It had become a booming private sector center for the production of cultivated black pearls, and this activity was strikingly successful compared to the aid agency projects. This is a business that is highly technical, but which islanders have managed to do very well. Half a million pearl shells, a third of which were seeded to produce black pearls, had the capacity to yield around US$2 million a year. Manihiki is blessed with a large lagoon reputed to be one of the most beautiful in the Pacific. It is also the home of the black-lip oyster (*Pinctada margaritifera*), which now provides the growth industry of the island and is the source both of promises and problems for its inhabitants. In 1991, everyone seemed to be in the pearl business.

None of the aid agencies had staff who knew much about the pearl industry, though they wanted to be involved in its success. Central government in Rarotonga was trying to assist the industry, but did not have an experienced cadre of staff in the Marine Resources Department. Local government, which received royalties from an expatriate producer who had a large farm in the lagoon, had borrowed around half a million dollars, but had not yet managed to purchase an office typewriter. Over US$120,000 had been spent by the Council on airfares for islanders to attend a celebration in Rarotonga. Lack of clean water, piles of rubbish everywhere, and rapidly increasing drunkenness and domestic violence were ignored by the Council. The Council was against the imposition of any local taxes.

The local member of Parliament, who was also the Minister for Marine Resources, believed that he, and the Marine Department under his control, ought to be the major player in the Outer Islands. The Mayor saw himself as standing up for the little people against the dangers of central government taxation. Both the politician and the Mayor wanted to dominate an industry but neither had the resources to assist in any significant technical manner.

The last stop on the officials' tour, Penrhyn, was known as "the island of the four evangelists." Missionaries had landed and converted the people in 1845. The missionaries then proceeded to sell the people to Peruvian slavers. The evangelists had even signed up to go as overseers to Peru to keep their flock in order. Penrhyn had received little development assistance since the U.S. army left in 1947, after constructing a deep-water wharf, an airfield, and a water system and connecting roads. People no longer produced copra. Cultivating pearls was banned from the lagoon, because the islanders feared that disease or surface-generated pollution would result. Fine hats were made, but to sell them profitably, it was necessary to go to Tahiti. Small, white, natural pearls, found in shells in the lagoon, were also sold. Nevertheless, a growing number of young men had no work and no hope of finding work. In families where there was no income at all, women traded hats, which they had woven, for food in the local store.

Men talked endlessly about making money, but had never actually done what they were talking about. Women spoke from experience. Women were the most entrepreneurial force for change. They had energy and drive. They made brooms and sold them. They wanted to make doughnuts and needed a machine. They wanted to make and sell more hats and more embroidered quilts. The officials from the global aid agencies, however, were not much interested in them, nor were the members of their local Councils.

A Tolerated Partnership

UN developers didn't get to know local people in the Cook Islands and local people saw no real reason to accept their advice if it involved work or changing what they felt comfortable doing. For their part, the UN officials felt that the way of life was so deficient that any changes they suggested should be welcomed. It is difficult for donors to accept that islands with blue translucent waters, white sandy beaches, waterfalls, wonderful flowers and butterflies, sensational birds, and friendly inhabitants should be allowed to produce such a poor standard of living for the people.

Cook Islanders must constantly deal with someone's idealized notion of how they should live. Tourists dislike the fact that the locals want to give up their charming, cool leaf huts for unsightly cement boxes with ugly corrugated iron roofing. Missionaries worry about alcoholism, wife-beating, and high suicide rates. Public health experts are concerned that Islanders don't swim for pleasure or even walk but instead prefer scooters.

The Cook Islanders were not concerned that donor projects failed because they didn't know that the aid agencies were supposed to be helping poor people. Nor did they care that the advice they got often failed to work. Most atoll dwellers live on the atolls because they like it there much better than living anywhere else. Even though those who want to leave do leave, the population is adequate.

They have survived generations of developers, and they will continue to do so. They willingly acquiesce in their dependency: it's a good deal for them and the developers. In return for aid money, which includes enough people from Europe and North America to do the tedious work that islanders don't like to do, the islanders are prepared to help the developers. If the donor projects fail, what have the islanders received from the donors? Thanks to aid agencies, Cook Islanders are among the world's most traveled people with burgeoning air miles accounts and a good sense of how to stretch their daily allowances provided by the aid agencies when they travel.

Reading

digim'Rina, Linus S. 2005. Food Security through Traditions: Replanting Trees and Wise Practices. People and Culture in Oceania 20:13–36.

Foster, Robert. 2002. Materializing the Nation: Commodities, Consumption, and Media in Papua New Guinea. Bloomington: Indiana University Press.

Gill, William Wyatt. 1984. From Darkness to Light in Polynesia. Apia, Western Samoa: University of the South Pacific, Commercial Printers.

Mair, Lucy P. 1948. Australia in New Guinea. London: Christophers.

Sahlins, Marshall D. 1963. Poor Man, Rich Man, Chief: Political Types in Melanesia and Polynesia. Comparative Studies in Society and History 5:285–303.

Scott, Dick. 1991. Years of the Pooh-Bah: A Cook Island History. Auckland: Hodder and Staughton.

Strathern, Andrew. 1982. Problems of Leadership and Communication in the Public Service in Papua New Guinea. Administration for Development 18:35.

Wynn, Barry. 1966. The Man Who Refused to Die. London: The Souvenir Press.

5

୨୨

Festival Elephant
Grandstanding in Tanzania

In the 1990s, Dar es Salaam residents could not drink the water, and moreover, the supply was frequently cut off. Electricity was often turned off in everyone's house by eight or nine in the morning and sometimes restored by six or seven at night. Tanzanians generally disliked Asians, and it was rumored that TANESCO, the power company, made those with Indian neighbors wait longer for their electricity to be restored. But that was probably beyond TANESCO's capacity.

Barabara mbaya sana is Kiswahili for a very bad road, and there were were many of them in Dar es Salaam and throughout the country. Often cratered with ponds two to four feet deep, rubble and mud everywhere, and no chance of anybody doing anything to improve them, these horrible, lurching, suspension-destroying roads were monuments to the results of former Prime Minister's Julius Nyerere's policy of self-reliance. Nyerere was elected president when (then) Tanganyika gained independence in 1961. He served from 1964 until 1985. He implemented a socialist economic program, called the Arusha Declaration, and instituted a policy of forced agricultural collectivization and village resettlement called Ujamaa. This policy, modeled loosely on the Chinese commune system, did not succeed. Nonetheless Nyerere, who brought together more than 120 diverse tribal groups into one country, is considered the "Father of the Nation."

Levels of violence in Dar were high, and robbery was pervasive. Robbers sometimes stole shoes, just shoes. Thieves stole from cars stopped at traffic lights or stuck in a big puddle. Backpackers were offered oranges that some kind soul had just peeled in front of them and then woke up naked without their possessions. The orange had been injected with a rather nasty drug. If anyone cut themself, you had to put on gloves first if you wanted to help because HIV/AIDS by this time had become common. With one person in four being HIV positive, it made sense for men to think carefully about the risks involved in visiting the barber.

In 1993, a coalition of donors including the World Bank, the United Nations Development Programme (UNDP), and Britain's Department for International Development offered me the job of Chief Advisor for Civil Service Reform in Tanzania. Some time after I had taken up my appointment I learned that the World Bank wanted to reduce the size and cost of the civil service. Other donors were in favor of having the civil service privatized; a few emphasized downsizing; and others thought it should be abolished. In discussions with donor representatives, I argued that the UNDP had made a fundamental mathematical error in calculating the size and growth of the civil service, and that it had overestimated growth by 400 percent. I expressed my concern that the donors' visions for reform did not include the possibility that there was something culturally distinctive about the Tanzanian civil service. They had a global view of what a civil service should be: the same everywhere.

I had other reservations about their approach. The donors made a serious error when they decided that it was more important to raise the salaries of those who worked within Tanzania's Central Bank, Ministry of Finance, and National Planning Commission, than the salaries of others in the country's civil service. Their decision weakened the idea that all civil servants were equally important.

The donors did little to combat the existing culture of corruption—a culture that had been in place for years. It had never effectively been challenged by the international agencies that held the purse strings, and never effectively complained about by nongovernmental organizations (NGOs), who also had the power to be heard. In the early 1990s, the most successful businesses in Tanzania were security firms selling protection and garages selling expensive cars to aid agency officials.

Corrupt practices involved both high-level and low-level employees. Bureaucratic corruption in Tanzania included bribery, extortion, speculation, absenteeism, and nepotism.

Historical Context

Tanganyika, taken over by the British from the Germans after World War I as a League of Nations Mandated Territory, received little British investment. It gained its independence before Kenya did, reflecting the confidence of Britain in Julius Nyerere. At the time of the country's independence, its infrastructure was poor, the number of high school and university graduates was small, and many of the public buildings and facilities, constructed by the Germans, were falling into a state of disrepair.

Donors often draw comparisons between Uganda and Tanzania (the name of the united territory of Tanganyika and Zanzibar created in 1963), both of which achieved independence in the early 1960s. They ask why can't Tanzania do as well as Uganda? By "doing well," they actually mean that the government of Uganda usually took their advice. They do not often mention that parliamentary democracy has not flourished in one of the donors' favorite countries. In fact, the two countries were in rather different situations at the time of their independence. Uganda was landlocked, had traditionally relied on coffee as a cash crop, and had to struggle to keep the peace among its major constituent tribal groups, as the tragic period of Idi Amin demonstrated. Uganda's success was probably due more to a good start and a boom in coffee prices than to enlightened donor advice or strong rule by current (2007) President Yoweri Museveni. British colonialism had been relatively kind to Uganda, the "pearl of Africa," a nickname implying its high value as a colonial jewel. Britain had sent experienced staff and had invested large sums of money in developing infrastructure and social services, such as health and education. So, Uganda, compared to Tanganyika, was in relatively good shape when it became independent.

In contrast, the British made some major mistakes in Tanganyika. During the late 1940s, senior people in the British government in London, who knew little about Africa, created massive farms for growing peanuts in order to supply essential vegetable oils to ease food rationing and restrictions in Britain caused by World War II. They thought that the Tanganyikans would adopt better farming practices if they could see the success of the huge farms. But by planting time in 1948, less than 10,000 acres of the brush had been cleared and rooted instead of the 3.5 million acres projected. The British government purchased four thousand tons of peanuts for seed in 1947, but only a fraction of this amount was actually planted. The ground was difficult to clear and few people wanted to clear it. After two years of effort, only 2,000 tons of peanuts had been harvested, 50 percent of what was purchased as seed.

In the years following independence, President Nyerere's experiments with socialism, and the forced resettlement of farming villages, ruined his country. This was not the way people wanted to live, and it was not the way that they wanted to work as farmers. The country became, and has been ever since, one of the world's poorest and one that is highly dependent on aid. Later, the war Tanzania waged against Uganda's Idi Amin after he had ousted Milton Obote as President probably ought not have been fought. It bankrupted the country and caused great hardship.

Experts on Tanzania view the Nyerere era as a disappointment in economic terms, though they recognize that impressive gains were made in the delivery of social services. Unfortunately, the social gains were not sustainable. President Nyerere's rhetoric about self-reliance masked a heavy reliance of the country on Chinese and Soviet aid. His policies destroyed the fabric of traditional society and put nothing workable in its place. Nyerere's slogan, *Uhuru na kazi* (freedom and work), turned into dependency and no work. The bottom was reached in 1983, following the breakdown of the East African Community, an intergovernmental association of three countries: Uganda, Kenya, and Tanzania. At this time, the people of Tanzania suffered badly from the lack of basic necessities including food, water, housing, and health and education services.

Chama Cha Mapinduzi (CCM) is the political party that has been in power in Tanzania since independence. The party, which has no significant opposition, provided strong support during the long presidency of Julius Nyerere. During this period, the civil service was, inevitably, politicized. Appointments and promotions, postings and terminations were all subject to CCM approval. The legislation establishing the State Planning Commission, which is still in force, made it clear that the role of planning was to serve the will of the party. In other ways, the party proved not much better or worse than other African single-party regimes. What surprises the outside observer of party politics in Tanzania is the fact that there has been so little politics. Unlike other countries, such as Nigeria, the politicians have been in power for a long time. For example, by early 1995 many of the Ministers in the government, including the Prime Minister, Mr. Msuya, had been in power for 20 to 25 years.

Tanzanian intellectuals increasingly criticized the one-party state following the reforms in the former Soviet Union in the 1990s. A commission proposed changes in the constitution that opened up the possibility of multi-party elections. The changes were adopted, and the first multi-party election was held at the local government level in October 1993 and in October 1994. Multi-party elections of the President and the National Assembly were held in October 1995. The reform of the political system has also included reduced state control of the media, making it possible for independent newspapers to exist.

In the 1990s, Tanzanian politicians viewed both global aid organizations and civil society organizations, particularly those that didn't give them much money, with deep suspicion. The politicians assumed that because they had been elected, they represented the will of the people. They assumed that any foreign organization should make an effort to find out what they, the politicians, wanted to do since they, the politicians, ought to know what the will of the people was. The politicians learned, to their fury, that the views of the international organizations rarely coincided with their opinion about how aid money should be spent.

Civil Service Reform

Civil service reform was part of the donor-inspired approach to "structural reform of the economy." The program in Tanzania started in 1984 with minor adjustments in the exchange rate and liberalization of trade and agriculture sector policies.

In the structural reform view, countries and their economic problems are not much different from household budgets. If more is being spent to repay existing loans and purchases than comes in from earnings, it is wise to consolidate debts in one big loan while borrowers attempt to put their house in order by controlling expenditures. On the expenditure side, countries were supposed to cut cost for a variety of programs, including civil service, public education, and public health. This is really what a structural adjustment program is all about. Tanzania got one of these debt-buster loans in 1986 and 1987 as a result of an agreement with the international agencies supported by the bilateral donors. Other debt buster loans followed. Unlike private citizens who overspend their household budgets, countries find that global aid agencies will still extend credit even when their house is not in order.

In 1986, the Government of Tanzania introduced an Economic Recovery Programme (ERP), followed by an Economic and Social Action Program (ESAP) in 1989. The Public Expenditure Review prepared in 1989 was the first document that analyzed the situation in the whole public sector. The Review addressed the need to eliminate subsidies to the parastatals (public enterprise companies owned by government supplying water, electricity, etc.), to review the functions of the government and to cut down the size of the civil service, to improve salaries, to reform the planning and budgeting system, and several other issues. The focus of reforms during the early 1990s was on macroeconomic management, reform of the financial system and of state-owned businesses. A new banking legislation was adopted and a state-owned Business Reform Commission was set up to lead the restructuring and divestiture of state-owned businesses.

The major idea shared by all the donors was that the Tanzanian civil service was too large and was expanding at an unsustainable rate (never mind that the number of the donor agency's Festival Elephants was doing the same). Moreover, the donors envisaged improvement in the main body of the civil service to be a consequence of paying higher salaries for top civil servants and providing nice offices for them. Other than these agreed-upon points, there were some divisions in thinking. The United Nations Development Programme wanted to control the Planning Ministry so they would be able to have control when it came to decide who got into what sectors and whose advice was accepted. The World Bank wanted to control the Ministry of Finance and the Central Bank. The British wanted to update the filing system.

The context in which these reforms were to be introduced, however, included a complex past and a deeply entrenched elite culture. During the Nyerere years, senior civil servants in Tanzania had learned to look after themselves. The elite, permanent secretaries, and a handful of senior people spend considerable official time and official resources generating extra income-earning opportunities, activities that are discreetly pursued. This strategy has a long history. During the difficult years of the later 1970s, civil servants used much of their official working time to secure a living wage. At the time, there was a shortage of goods accompanied by the deterioration of the real value of salaries, which started in the mid-1970s. The elite in government, state commercial enterprises, and the Party enjoyed better access to the scarce goods than others.

Few of the elite civil servants made it their business to meet with a broad cross section of the people. Most restricted their contact to others of a similar rank. Paperwork in the civil service became a matter of external relations. Senior civil servants were no longer so interested in the performance of their junior staff or in contacts with the public; that concern had been replaced with a higher priority—pleasing the donors. Tanzania has an elite class whose members are acutely conscious of their power and standing. They are very bright, much brighter than the politicians for whom they have an affectionate contempt.

During the Nyerere years, when the economy was struggling, many of the Tanzanian elite left the country on overseas postings and assignments. Their children were educated overseas and their orientation, and increasingly the orientation of their parents, is toward overseas rather than toward their home country, and certainly not toward the village. The practice of educating the children overseas has continued, and a whole pattern of behavior is in place that indicates that the elite doubt that there is a future for their children in Tanzania.

The elite tell stories in the Dar es Salaam "Leaders Club." They have the inside gossip on banking, privatization, civil service reform, donor positions, local government, and investment proposals. Their sense of humor is very well developed when it comes to corruption: "Ah, that one. He was good. When he went overseas he had shelves inside his overcoat."

Global Aid Feeding Frenzy

The donors argued that tax administration must be quickly improved. They thought that the people responsible for collecting and handling large sums of money should be paid well if they were to do their jobs well, and if they were to be shielded from temptation. Consequently, Tanzanian officials working in institutions that the major donors favored, such as the Central Bank and the Ministries of Finance and Planning, and the Environment, were given excellent terms and conditions of service and opportunities that set them apart from officials in other institutions. This move sent a signal to the civil service that to get ahead you had to have more money.

It seemed to me a totally impractical idea that poor countries should be told that the only way you could expect public service was to pay more to the government. Surely, there was something else that could have been done to encourage public service. Would Cuba have been able to build a good medical service on this basis? Would Sri Lanka have been able to build a good educational system? If these countries could get public service only by paying more, then the outlook was grim. In Tanzania, most young high school graduates, and even school dropouts, wanted to become customs officials, because this was the job that yielded big money quickly.

Tanzanians have a saying that donors should have heeded: a fish rots from the head down. Aid officials in Tanzania assumed that the money they poured in at the top of government would trickle down to the poor. Instead, as they poured more and more money into the top, corrupt officials simply siphoned off more than before. Nothing was left to trickle down to anywhere near the poor. All across the government, officials were figuring out how to get a share of this new money. The immigration authorities worked out a clever scheme. They instituted a process of questioning expatriates a few weeks after they had arrived in Tanzania, asking them to produce their marriage license. Since few people ever keep such a document, many expatriates found themselves in a situation where they either had to pay a fine of US$100 or face a deportation order.

When global aid agencies complained that several hundred million dollars in revenues had not been collected, the government issued a stern warning to civil servants in revenue generating departments. They invented a wonderful phrase, "unjust enrichment," to describe what they wanted to stamp out. Of course, if you close one rabbit hole another one usually opens. There were so many opportunities and rewards. An officer in the Ministry of Finance had children in a well-known public school in Britain that charged fees that were in excess of 30 times his annual salary. When you went to ask for your electricity bill, you might be very politely asked what sort of a bill you wanted. He meant it. A small bribe to him and you could have the bill you wanted.

Some senior Tanzanian officials rented out their houses for several thousand dollars a month to expatriates and then claimed official quarters complete with domestic servants, drivers, gardeners, and telephone service all paid for by the state. Global aid agencies that were promoting new standards in the civil service saw nothing wrong in Permanent Secretaries having these irregular perquisites: It was a matter of tradition, of status. The aid relationship was helped by financial lubrication. Local officials received allowances and honorariums, and even salary supplements from global aid agencies for simply doing the job the government paid them to do. Then there were cars and computers, scholarships for children, as well as travel to exotic places. These perks created a relationship between aid agency officials and senior civil servants, but not a healthy one.

In 1992, the donors decided to lay off 50,000 staff and to use the money saved from these salaries to top up the salaries of those who remained. Donor economists pointed out that no tax was paid on allowances and so paying civil servants in allowances rather than straight salary represented not only a loss of revenue but also a lost opportunity for civil servants to build up their pensions. What was not said was that donors had no more intention of giving up their tax-free allowances than any Tanzanian official. Although donors paid millions of dollars in rents every year to landlords and the landlords paid no tax on the receipts, the donors would not pass the names of the landlords to the Inland Revenue service at the Treasury. I argued in vain that this massive retrenchment did not make sense. The commitment and energy of a civil servant was not the result of a pay raise or productivity agreement; it was not an outcome of cost-cutting or reorganization or rationalization or downsizing. Many things had to happen: leadership, lacking at the top of the civil service, would have to be shown. No such luck.

The Tanzanians had no choice other than to agree with the donors' plan if they wanted their next slice of structural adjustment money from the World Bank. But they had no intention of retrenching those at the top of the civil service, even though retrenching these people would have produced a large sum for redistribution. Instead, they fired all the people at the bottom of the civil service. The amount saved on salaries was negligible.

As I watched the nonsense over downsizing and the relative lack of concern among aid officials for the consequences of what they were doing, I was reminded of what Tolstoy wrote about some of the people who work for the "public good" in *Anna Karenina*:

> . . . Levin regarded his brother as a man of immense intellect and culture, as generous in the highest sense of the word, and possessed of a special faculty for working for the public good...The better he knew his brother, the more he noticed that Sergey Ivanovitch and many other people who worked for the public welfare, were not led by an impulse of the heart to care for the public good, but reasoned from intellectual considerations that it was the right thing to take interest in public affairs, and consequently took interest in them. Levin was confirmed in this generalization by observing that his brother did not take questions concerning the public welfare or the question of the immortality of the soul a bit more to heart than he did chess problems, or the ingenious construction of a new machine (1950:283).

In 1992, I argued, eventually successfully, that local government should be an important part of civil service reform. Local government, which should have been playing a critical role in poverty alleviation, had been banned for twelve years without any great pressure to reinstate it from the donors. Some years after the abolishment of local governments, it was clear that the reform had failed in the municipalities, and urban councils were reintroduced in 1978. Later, in 1982, a Local Government Act was passed and district councils were revived. These reforms did not, however, affect the regional administration in any significant way. The development planning system based on village, ward, district, and regional development committees was maintained. The administration and council level was also mainly kept unchanged. Although given certain powers to collect revenue, the councils from the start depended heavily on grants from the central government to finance their operations. During the colonial era, local councils had raised 98 percent of their expenditures from their own resources. By 1995, they raised only 2 percent of their expenditures.

Bypassing Tanzanian Culture

In the 1990s, neither the resident aid agency staff in Dar es Salaam nor the senior donor officials who visited for a few weeks at a time ever got to know the country, its people, and their rich cultural traditions in any depth. Global aid agency staff was not, and still is not, required to learn the major language of Tanzania, Kiswahili. Aid officials, both resident staff and the periodic visitors on mission, acted as if an invisible shield stood between them and the people and culture of Tanzania. Their invisible shield blocked them from hearing or heeding Tanzanians' advice, exhortations, public policy pronouncements, and appeals for support and funds. Their confidence in the Myth of Global Poverty and global programs meant that they needed to waste none of their precious time learning about poverty within the Tanzanian context or ever making personal contact with poor people.

During this period, global aid agencies began to hire increasing numbers of highly paid consultants who were assigned to work in their developing country offices. Most consultants were economists and accountants educated in Europe and the United States, but they had no training and little interest in the local context. Big international accounting firms, such as Coopers & Lybrand and Touche Ross, maintained impressive, well-staffed offices in Tanzania. Ironically, to help with the lucrative business of privatization during the early 1990s, these firms often employed many of the very same expatriate consultants who had earlier, in the 1960s, advised on how the state could take over private sector assets. The big accounting firms ambitiously claimed to deal with any issue where large sums of money were involved: providing healthcare, maintaining museums, administering justice, imposing taxes, expanding trade, growing flowers, floating shares, and sinking funds.

Meanwhile, in the government ministries in Dar es Salaam, the corridors and stairwells were dank and dark, the windows broken, and working elevators scarce to nonexistent. The phones didn't work and neither did the toilets. Supplicants lined the open spaces, waiting for hours to see someone who might help them, clearly conscious of their powerlessness.

Junior bureaucrats trudged along muddy streets on their way to work in a tropical downpour, trying to keep the few clothes they owned presentable. Civil servants were housed inadequately and paid terribly. Many worked in dilapidated, drab offices with not enough chairs and tables, let alone office equipment and supplies, to go around.

Donors siphoned off all the best local talent, and were on the lookout for more. Credentials were the order of the day. Graduate degrees were an automatic ticket to a good job with the expatriates.

Poverty and What to Do about It

In Kiswahili, the counterpart to the English word "poverty" is not "having no money" but instead "having no family." This meaning originates in the period of time before the introduction of the cash economy in the nineteenth century. Even now, for Tanzanians and many other African peoples, the family group is the crucial unit that ensures well-being and security. In the family, wage-earners support those who have no work. Family members share food and shelter with immediate members as well as more distant family who may fall on hard times and knock on the door seeking assistance. The costs of schooling, health, marriage, and death all involve extensive family member interactions and financial sharing. The process of raising funds for a marriage or funeral brings the group together, cementing ties and creating future obligations. Families, as locally defined, are large, and obligations and security networks diffuse.

To be alone in Tanzania was to be "poor", because as long as you had someone to look out for you when you needed shelter, food, or healthcare, you would be fine within the context of your society. In the 1990s, traditional arrangements for helping the poor no longer worked because Nyerere had broken up the tribal groupings with his village programs, and the modern arrangements failed to work. The terrible scourge of AIDS in Africa reinforced this point. AIDS made demands on family support structures and, once these structures were gone, this support was hard to replace. But the afflicted continued to look for this support, which was why, sadly, so many urban dwellers went home to die in their ancestral villages.

Waziri's boss fired him early that morning for being late. Getting fired wasn't supposed to happen during Ramadan because Muslims believe that any bad deeds done during that special time would receive extra punishment. He was late because the police had stopped him, asking to see his pass, which was the code for a bribe. He didn't have the money, and so they beat him up, which made him late to work.

He couldn't go to his home village because he had no relatives there who could support him. Now over 40, he had worked several years as a driver but he had developed cataracts and found it difficult to see. He hadn't been able to get another job for more than a year.

When the rains came that year, the floor of his house was covered with water, some of it contaminated. There were no proper toilets in this densely populated area of Dar, which was beside a river. In the dry season, the dust and the smell from the sewer were terrible. In the rainy season, there were more mosquitoes and malaria. He had only one shirt and two pairs of shorts. His family of six children had been given mosquito nets by a church group, but he had to sell them. The cots were stacked one on another because their room was too small for all the children to spread out. The children had nightmares ever since robbers had stolen their pots and pans. The children rummaged through the nearby rubbish dump to find aluminum cans or plastic bags to sell for small amounts of cash. Sometimes the children stole food from stalls. Often, they went hungry for many days. They had no light at night because they couldn't afford either electricity or kerosene.

His previous wife had died from a disease. His brother also died, and Waziri wasn't able to get the body from the morgue because the men would not release it without payment.

The poor next look for help from their tribe, and, even more widely, from those who are from the same region. People from one's region may assist with a job. The country is made up of twenty-eight distinctive tribal groups of which none comprises more than 12 to 14 percent of the overall population. Tribal assistance, however, declined due to President Nyerere's attempts to reduce tribal ties and identity. Socialism and Nyerere's Ujaama program uprooted people from their home regions and tribes, dispersing them all over the country.

Global poverty thinking assumed that aid agencies and governments of developing countries would be the principal vehicles for assistance for the global poor. But in Tanzania, the poor don't look to aid agencies for help. One reason for this situation is that the agencies and their staff were out of sight in Dar es Salaam. Another factor is that helping the poor was not something that the Tanzanian government was motivated to do. And, in fact, it was not something that citizens expected them to do. Asking officials for help could be pointless in a country where simple medical care was either dangerous or highly expensive, and where food was scarce or beyond people's means. In Tanzania, some help for the poor did come from the Red Cross, the Aga Khan Foundation, and the Red Crescent, as well as from churches and missionary organizations and civil society organizations. But the needs of the poor were so great that these well-meaning efforts barely scratched the surface of the country's poverty problems.

Yet, everything aid agencies did in Tanzania in the 1990s had a poverty label stuck on it. Poverty justified and supported the Festival Elephant performance. It is not surprising that projects with a poverty label rarely worked. One example of a failed project with surprising unintended (and negative) consequences was a birth control program that the UNDP said had done well in other countries. The local agency office thought there was no need to delay implementing the project in Tanzania by doing fieldwork, interviews, and a pilot project. The Myth of Global Poverty says to start a project by moving money. In the early phase of the project, agency representatives were delighted to find that demand for birth control pills was increasing. They were, at the same time, perplexed that the birth rate in the target area was not dropping.

One evening, project staff met a veterinarian who explained why he thought some of the women receiving the pills were using them since they were not interested in having fewer children. The owner of a cat brought the animal to him with signs of pregnancy, but he knew he had operated on it to prevent that from happening a few weeks previously. He learned that the cat's owner had been feeding it chicken scraps. He also learned that people had fed birth-control pills to the chickens. Women found that adding the pills to the chicken feed produced a nice plump bird in a short time. Since the pills were supplied in industrial quantities, there was a plentiful supply of chicken feed. So the chickens ate the pills and grew plump as did the cat that ate the chicken scraps. But children also were eating the chickens fed with birth control pills, and consequently young boys began to grow noticeable breasts.

If the donors wanted to reach all the poor people in the country, then they had to be able to show the government how this could be done and how poverty alleviation could be afforded. But donor projects were far too expensive for the government to be able to afford to provide them for all poor people. Donor-designed projects didn't show the government what to do because these projects needed above average advantages such as motivated and educated participants who were already well-off, armies of expensive overseas consultants, high-level political support, lots of expatriates, and unusually high local salaries. This was not a model that a government could follow in order to alleviate mass poverty.

A remarkable thing about the Tanzanians was how they put up with so much that has not worked from those who were supposed to be helping them. They were notably tolerant, in general, of differences: different religions, different ethnicity, and different social outlooks. Yet these were the same people who were quick to anger when they caught a thief—who would likely be stoned to death as punishment. In Dar es Salaam, thieves were increasingly punished by setting fire to rubber motor tires that were put around the thief's neck.

Relationships with Festival Elephants in Dar

Aid officials from Britain, the United States, Canada, France, Germany, Japan, and the Scandinavian countries were housed in their country's embassies and given diplomatic status. In Tanzania, the government treated the heads of global aid agencies in the same way as the heads of diplomatic missions from the same countries. In a short time, by 1993, the aid officials were accustomed to being treated as ambassadors and diplomats. The World Bank representative acted as if he were the most powerful person in the city. The UNDP representative liked to be driven round town with his UN flag fluttering. Even heads of civil society organizations acquired duty-free imports and tax exemption privileges. Top-level aid people lived in houses as grand as those of other ("real") ambassadors. Likewise, they were invited to diplomatic parties and receptions. When making brief visits to project sites, they traveled comfortably in special trains, boats, and planes in their role as special development voyeurs.

In contrast to the Festival Elephant aid officials, many of the regular diplomats were closer to real life in Tanzania. They took the trouble to try to learn the language and something about Tanzania. They spent more time traveling to remote areas than the aid personnel and were more in touch with people from all walks of life.

In order to maintain a position as the highest or second highest per capita recipient of aid funds in the world, senior Tanzanian civil servants developed skills to manage their relationships with donors. These skills produce masses of aid money and goods, but nothing in the way of uncomfortable change.

Tanzanians wanted the money, and donor personnel wanted to demonstrate to their superiors that their agency was making progress or was just about to make progress. The Tanzanians sensed, quite rightly, that the donors did not want to see their favorite ideas on global poverty fail. So the Tanzanians graciously continued to offer support even when things went wrong. When an ambitious expatriate finds that she or he has inherited, or supported, a beautifully executed but terribly wrong project, a way out is needed. Tanzanians are there to lend a helping hand. Young expatriates want their headquarters assured that they could do the job. They need a good word in a senior visitor's ear to help secure a new job or a promotion. The collaboration between the donors and Tanzanian officials kept the Festival Elephants performing.

When donors criticize the Tanzanians at international meetings for poor revenue collection or corruption, the Tanzanians quietly accept the blame. They are good sports. They murmur "pole sana," an elegant Kiswahili expression of condolence. They know from experience that even when donors get angry with them, they still care. In other words, there is thus still more money to be had. They also know there is reluctance on the part of donors to admit that they don't know the answers. Thus Tanzanians do not have to come to terms with sorting out their own affairs because the donors have never had to come to terms with their own spectacular mistakes. The performance now involved expatriates and Tanzania officials in a long-term play of denial as both parties are seduced by the Myth of Global Poverty and the cash flow at the top that it generates.

"Love letters" between donors and Tanzanian officials kept the romance going. When my friend from the Ministry of Finance in Tanzania bought the first beer, I knew he must be excited. He shouted at me, because the bar at the Kilimanjaro hotel in Dar es Salaam was a little crowded. "Ah, Chief Advisor," he said (my title was Chief Advisor for Civil Service Reform), "Why are your donors writing us love letters?" His colleagues from the Ministry of Finance grinned good-humouredly. Very odd, I thought, and tried to drink my beer quietly. I wondered if his excitement would run to his buying a second beer; that would really have been a red-letter day.

The letter had been written at agency headquarters in the U.S. as part of the ongoing structural adjustment dialogue between Tanzania and the World Bank and the other donors. It praised the courage of the government in addressing civil service and public enterprise reform. The government had shown the kind of leadership that other countries in the region needed. Their commitment to the poor was outstanding. The letter went on to promise and pledge continuing assistance if the government continued with the reforms. Good news for the government, which penned a passionate reply to the donors.

Love letters? Of course these were love letters. Writers of love letters are licensed to make extravagant promises that both the writer and the recipient know will never come to pass—this is what writing love letters is all about. None of what the donors said was true; we knew it and the government knew it. Writing love letters to the government saved face. The donors could continue the myth that their money and ideas were producing results, and the government could get more money without having to make any painful changes or provide "the dog ate my homework" sort of excuse. After exchanging the love letters, the funds that the government wanted and that the agencies wanted to give them, were released with the usual disappointing result.

Festival Elephants as Shadow Government

Aid agency staff took decisions that in their own countries would be the preserve of politicians when they determined the kind of education or health services that would be provided or what sort of public transport would be made available. Beginning in the 1980s, Tanzania was the beneficiary of policy-based lending, sometimes involving loans of several hundred million dollars. This vast amount of money was used to persuade the government to change policies or to draft new policies to benefit the poorest, in return for which finance was provided. Disbursement usually continued in instances where less than half of the conditions laid down were met. As the donors financed more and more of the running and ruining of Tanzania, they also kept wringing their hands and protesting that they want to serve the public good. Although aid agencies cooperated on some issues, they competed on others. Each pushed and shoved to persuade the government to grant access to a prized sector, such as healthcare or education. In a way, things had not moved on a great deal since the missionaries used to divide up a country into spheres of influence. As James Ferguson shows in the case of Lesotho, the aid agencies there had more of an impact on politics in the recipient country than they did on poverty alleviation.

Each year, the aid agencies cranked out reports on the Tanzanian economy and on the status of various projects. These documents, rather than leading to positive changes for the poor in Tanzania, determined the success of the career of individual agency staff. The documents also provided a basis for the public reputation of the agencies and support for their receiving continued and enhanced resources in the future. Several hundred of these documents were produced each year. Tanzania hosted hundreds of aid agency missions or team visits. It was important for the careers of agency staff that they had led important missions to recipient countries.

When aid agency staff arrived at one of the main hotels in the capital on mission, they always had an air of slight impatience. They seemed taut, like the G-string on a violin. They were in constant staccato motion rushing through the hotel with files and folders. They sent and received faxes. Backwards and forwards they paced about importantly, as if on military maneuvers in a vast unknown country. They had a constant need for meetings with each other. In meetings, they sat as if they were tournament chess players. Underneath the table, limbs were writhing and wrapped around table legs. Above the table, the bodies did not betray the slightest twitch. They wrote important things on yellow legal pads. Each took care not to talk too much, not to laugh too much. They demonstrated focus. They were polite to hotel staff, but not friendly. Each morning and each evening, they ate together and exchanged information.

Their rituals of work were impressive. Reports dripped with data, tables, and boxes that were seldom read or closely examined. Each year, the volume of statistical data increased as if in response to some obsessive hopes that it could create meaning where none existed. The tone was always measured, judgments reasoned, conclusions orthodox. There was no question of including anything not backed up by data or numbers.

The formidable mission weaponry was always aimed at Tanzania as the problem. Aid officials never considered that their own agency actions or the actions of other donors were part of the problem. The standard for the thinking and the presentation was the same no matter what subject the mission was assessing. Novelty was not encouraged. The aim was not to set new standards that might be seen as an implied criticism of senior management; the objective was to meet standards already established. There was no question of intellectual partnership between mission members and Tanzanians. The mission's view was global, all-powerful, and not to be questioned.

What mattered to staff was that their superiors noticed the skill with which they assisted the process of project bombardment, their inventiveness in getting agreement on large loans, the incisiveness of their analytical papers—but not the warmth and depth of their relationships with local people. The emphasis on the quantity of projects approved and money moved is reminiscent of a story told by the novelist George Santayana. When teaching at Harvard, he was stopped one day at the beginning of term by the President of the College, who asked him how things were going. Santayana prattled on about the sort of student who was doing well, how nice they were, and so on. A look of irritation came over the President's face as he said: "I meant how many do you have in your class?"

Dealing with Donors

It was a challenge for the Tanzanians, in the capital as well as in rural areas, to undertake all the cross-cultural journeys required in order to deal with the donors, their ideas, and their activities.

During the 1990s, aid agency personnel poured into Tanzania, chanting mantras about stabilizing the currency, transparency, reducing the functions of the state, governance, sustainable development, safeguarding the environment, and structural adjustment. In addition, the donors exposed Tanzanians to a constantly changing cast of many international characters including more expatriates than international private sector business used.

Tanzania has hosted planners trained in Russia; New Zealanders anxious to manage the public sector like a business; Australian stockmen, highly concerned that locals be taught how to put up a stout fence; Canadians fascinated by agricultural engineering; Polish advisors from the United Nations Industrial Organization, determined to demonstrate their understanding of computer technology; Indian economists poised to show what their discipline can do; Sri Lankan accountants who are sticklers for procedures; Americans who want to harness satellite technology; Pakistanis who believe that a good Civil Service Staff College could solve many problems; Chinese engineers trying to construct Olympic facilities or some other symbol of everlasting friendship, very quickly and very cheaply; Germans, trying to reproduce the "dual training" partnership they have known between industry and public institutions; Irish, showing what their Industrial Development Authority thinking can do; Finns building, equipping, staffing, and training entire hospitals or chipboard factories; Japanese, anxious to grow rice or produce a master plan of something important for the future where their private sector construction or engineering industry can play a prominent role; British graduates—with no charity or social work background—prepared to eliminate or halve poverty; Swedes starting Folk Colleges. In addition there may be Baptists running an adoption business and NGOs engaged in environmental campaigns.

It is useful to see what life is like for important government officials and how they handle the donors. Let us follow a Tanzanian Permanent Secretary for a day.

James Deighton's family, wanting to give him a good start in life, named him after the last four missionaries who had visited their village. He was the only Cambridge man at a senior level in the Tanzanian government. When Nyerere was in power, there had been several. Many of his colleagues now were graduates of Patrice Lumumba University in Moscow or some Chinese institution whose name he could not remember.

The Ministry of Finance was housed in a wooden structure of two floors, sporting a wide wrought-iron balcony on the second floor, and topped with a rusty corrugated iron roof. Deighton's office almost faced the sea. It had high ceilings and a single fan with one working speed. In the office sat some substantial Colonial-era furniture, which looked as sound as the day it had been built. Split-cane furniture with worn, stained green cushions stood in each corner. The desk was solid mahogany and quite serviceable when he made sure that the rock under the shorter of the legs was in place. His chair was large and vinyl-covered and quite attractive if you could stop the stuffing oozing out of the bottom.

Inside the wooden bookcase with its glass-fronted doors were piles of old Gazettes and a few law books; these, James found, were, totally illegible because of termites, though only a few years old.

The Ministry building was surrounded by what had once been a lawn. In the middle was a flagpole. The lawn was long gone, since people liked to sit on the ground, park cars and vans there, or make small fires for cooking meals. The police used to raise a flag each morning, but they had given up that practice as a sign of displeasure over budget cuts. The Ministry was a good spot to meet with prospective donors, since they could see that this was not a country that was wasting money.

The Ministry was always crowded. People came to bid on contracts, because this was where the Government Tender Board was. For those who played by the rules, the Tender Board Box was a small wooden container on the first floor, into which contractors and vendors placed their sealed bids.

Soundproofing the office was one of the first things Deighton did when he was appointed. Given some of the conversations he had, this seemed wise. Deighton had known that visitors lolling in the chairs outside the Secretary's office could hear what was going on inside. Deighton was not only the man who put the budget together; he was also the Price Controller. More than one merchant had, in the past, made a killing on what he had heard through those walls. Grace, his secretary, was no beauty, but that was not why he had hired her. She was his wife's niece and could be expected to look out for his interests when she could tear herself away from talking to young men on the phone. Her coffee-making was not too bad, and she was beginning to remember to put six spoons of sugar in his mug. She could always be counted on to produce, no matter how many, all the cups and saucers he needed for a meeting. She was also good at getting biscuits. Pity they didn't do that sort of thing in the rich countries he visited.

People came to get payments, to demand payments, or just to see if they or any of their relatives were entitled to payments. Relatives came to collect their share when it was payday for an employee of the ministry. A few reluctant souls even came to make payments to the government.

He was responsible for attending over 200 board meetings by virtue of his position. He didn't want to delegate until he at least knew what the problems were. Other government departments and people in the private sector didn't want to deal with his staff; they were slighted if he didn't take care of them personally. First attempts at delegation had been a disaster. Several very poorly thought-through papers had been sent to Cabinet and Cabinet sent him a rocket. Then the Cabinet demanded that the Secretary of Finance be in attendance at all Cabinet meetings, which meant that office hours grew longer. The financial section in the Ministry that had not been sorted out because of all the other disasters going on at the same time, had completely underestimated government revenues and had gone out and borrowed to cover the shortfall. Without asking him, they had borrowed in Swiss francs and the Swiss franc had already appreciated over 10 percent against the local currency.

Deighton met with his top staff to review again what needed to be done. The conference room table was long and covered with a piece of glass, which magnified the cigarette burns underneath. The walls were paneled with local hardwood, a gesture his predecessor had made in hopes of impressing some visiting private sector industrialist. A massive Chubb safe adorned with Queen Victoria's coat of arms stood in one corner. Visitors from the bush were often told that it was where the government kept its money. The only blessing agreed on by all experienced attendees of meetings in this room was that it was so hot that lengthy meetings were impossible.

He began briskly: "My dears, I think it best that we have a clear understanding about our problems. The donors are suggesting that we are badly behind in our work. They say that the Prime Minister wants a greatly expanded goods and services target and accelerated investment. We can't handle the work that we now have, let alone take on new tasks. But I'd like to give you a chance to show what you can do. We'll just try to soldier on."

Festival Elephants Facing Each Other

At the same time, the many expatriates involved in the aid business in Tanzania had to try to deal with each other's cultural differences. The French love grey areas and are, after all, a people excellently suited for policy. They define things to the point where they gain some advantage. But they are likely to be frustrated by the Germans, a people whose representatives often insist on being like their stereo-types. Germans, who tend to have a paternalistic view of manage-ment, like to have an important role in meetings and thus often begin with the conclusions. Americans have a keen interest in introducing business methods to government, but are horrified at the thought of an inefficient civil servant being allowed anything like the perks con-sidered normal for a private sector executive, even in a business los-ing money.

One morning in the German embassy, Dieter Genz looks at himself again in the window of his office. He plays with his moustache and moves his head so that the profile looks more like that of his old profes-sor at Heidelberg whom he admires as a successful person. Why were things going so slowly for Dieter Genz? German or Swiss companies could be persuaded to offer him a job, but what he really wanted was an academic position. He was, however, getting out of touch.

At this time of the year one could meet old friends while skiing. Dieter gazes at himself in the window again. If only he could find time to do some leg exercises, it would make skiing so much easier. A loss of 4 or 5 kilos would help. Nevertheless, he did look pretty good on the slopes.

He believes that consultants were like lice: they would eat the hair off your head! He didn't like paying them all that money. It was easy, though, to get policy research going at HQ and it would be low cost, because there was an inexhaustible supply of bright young men who would do anything to get a chance of a permanent appointment at HQ. The useful thing about the aspiring young people was that they could be asked to help with all the work, and their services could be billed to the policy proj-ects. The research assistants would not complain because they knew that complaints might mean that they were out for good.

Dieter's most serious problem, which he had managed to conceal amazingly well, was that he could not write in English. Research assis-tants wrote his letters and memos. When he had to produce a draft, he used a dictaphone but that didn't always work very well, even though he had chosen his secretary precisely because she had indicated that she could help with that kind of thing.

Like many Germans, Dieter never learned as a young boy to say "please" or "thank you" even though there are such words in German. His commanding language infuriated the family he lived with in Britain— "pass the butter" never went down very well with them. Dieter's solution to this linguistic and cultural problem in later life was to look very grave and to begin the most peremptory and inconsiderate of requests with "would you be so kind as to?"

Dieter was an observant person. This morning he made calls to all the people with whom he needed, to keep in touch if he were ever to get a better job back home. He made an average of 15 to 20 calls a day to Europe, some of which were about business. But today was his mother's birthday. Instead of putting the call through himself, he had his secretary do it for him. His mother was thrilled when he told her he would be home for Christmas. Ach, for Schlachtplatte.

When one UN staff member replaced another overseas, one could not expect the successor to have the same work habits, the same way of doing things, the same instruction pedagogy, the same view of discipline, the same view of effort, the same view of incentives, and the same way of managing. A Russian official succeeded a Filipino official and so on. A poor country had to accommodate to the view of management and procedures held by individuals, each of whom wished to make her or his mark on development in Tanzania. I dealt with a Korean, a man from the Netherlands, a Dane, several Swedes, a Thai national, a Kenyan, a man from Trinidad, a Scot, a woman from London, and an American, all of whom had different ideas about what Civil Service Reform should do. They wanted to keep on top of developments by making a two week trip to Tanzania two or three times a year.

Increasing Aid, a Failing State, and Rising Poverty

By the 1990s, the system of public education had collapsed. Education for all was a myth, promoted by donors in countless documents and believed by no one. One child in seven of those who ought to have been in primary school actually attended, and over the previous ten years literacy had slipped from over 90 percent to around 60 percent. Exam results were very bad and worrying for parents. As part of the World Bank's structural adjustment programs, schools began charging fees. Per term, these fees amounted to a month's wages for a manual worker. Some teachers, whose salaries were delayed by many months, would teach only those pupils who actually handed over cash in excess of the fees. Those who did not pay were not taught. Pupils also had to pay to have exams marked and those that did not pay did not get their exams marked. In most instances in any case, there were no materials in schools, particularly in rural areas, for teachers to use, or no books for children.

Despite massive evidence relating to preschooling and educational disadvantage and special needs, education was failing. Primary school education reflected another global program, and that program was the successor to a belief that vocational education would be the savior of poor countries. Eventually, it was concluded that vocational education did not represent the best use of funds, and all children should go to primary school. Where their pet ideas were concerned, such as the importance of universal primary education, aid officials could get quite snippy with local officials if they felt they were not doing enough. Some years later, the aid agencies realized that improvement was a much more comprehensive affair involving not only primary but also secondary and tertiary education.

"You realize," said the aid official with a look that indicated that he doubted that Samson Yamboah understood, "that sending one student to university means that 348 girls do not go to primary school?" Samson is a 30-year-old Tanzanian who studied development at the University of London. His ambition was to work for an international agency so that he could see more of the world.

Samson's attempt to say something was cut-off by a short outburst from another aid official to the effect that the figures showed that the returns from primary education should be the highest in the educational system. However, at present, school achievement was very low. According to the global aid agency calculus, school attendance was down because parents were consumers who were choosing to not pay for a poor quality product. All that had to be done to improve achievement and enrollment was to raise the quality. Make teachers work longer hours. Reduce the number of teachers. Raise the salaries of the remaining teachers to provide the necessary motivation.

Samson's assistant passed him a piece of paper: "Point out that the expensive university is a result of advice from previous officials. Girls and the teachers are tired all day because they have been told to make their schools financially self-sufficient by growing all their own food. They have to walk to school. Girls are small and weak for their age since they suffer from malnutrition. Attendance will not improve because parents withdraw their children at puberty—an educated girl who is spoiled by being made pregnant by her teacher is of less value than an uneducated girl with good marriage prospects."

Samson shook his head. No, he couldn't say that. These aid officials had never been to the remote rural areas. They wouldn't know what he was talking about. As Principal Secretary, and thus an important person, Samson was upset by this peremptory treatment. The international aid officials had been so rude to him in front of junior officers that he had forgotten to introduce his staff.

The children of the poor did not have toys, let alone access to reading material. No toys to play with may have meant that a whole series of motor skills might be underdeveloped as a child grows up. This might have had something to do with the fact that you couldn't easily find an electrician to wire a plug or a watchmaker who could do delicate work.

Medical services were also breaking down due to the strain of dealing with a lack of supplies and low salaries. As of 1992, a million HIV-positive cases were too great for existing administrative systems. In Kagera, in the northeastern part of the country, no regular medical services existed. Doctors and nurses were not posted to the region because staff feared that they would contract AIDS. Sadly, there appeared to be no need to downsize the army. Given the HIV/AIDS situation, half of the people in the army were likely to be dead within five years.

People living in remote rural areas had fewer working visits from agricultural extension and supervisory staff than they had in the 1940s and 1950s. On paper, it often looked as if field visits were increasing. In reality, the visits were fictitious, logged in for the money that could double or triple a civil servant's take-home pay.

Lack of a sense of service and accountability pervaded many sectors. Poor people expressed bitterness over the quality of service provided by nurses. Yet, out of 25,000 nursing personnel, only two or three were dismissed year after year. Traffic police openly shook down drivers in the middle of the day. Other police brazenly solicited for bribes at the airport. Principal secretaries, who had up to four thousand "ghosts" (employees who did not exist) on the payroll in their department, did not receive a letter of reprimand. A Presidential party on a three-day visit to Copenhagen spent over US$300,000.

I asked the officer in charge of a revenue office in Dar es Salaam why several billion shillings—US$4 to 6 million—had not been banked. Great bundles of notes were stacked up in a massive open safe that dated back to the time the Germans had run the country. I pointed out that if this money were banked regularly, government might not have to borrow so much each day to pay bills. They should be concerned about security—what if robbers came? "Mzee," [old one], said the officer in charge, "I do not have the money to buy the rubber bands for the notes and the bank will not accept loose notes."

Enter Civil Society Organizations and More Festival Elephants

The civil society organizations that have proliferated since the 1970s have become powerful international organizations. When I was working in Tanzania, I was struck by the irony that many civil society organizations quickly became mirror images of the global aid agencies, in spite of their ostensible opposition to the way that those aid agencies worked.

Like the global aid agencies, large civil society organizations such as CARE and Oxfam began to adopt the Myth of Global Poverty and hire their own Festival Elephants who prance around telling everyone what they should do. They, too, have neglected to build cultural competence. There are, however, lessons to be learned from some of the smaller, more grassroots civil society organizations. Their staff, often made up of local people, is trained in anthropological skills, have local cultural competence, respect local people, and spend time with local people listening to and learning from them, and building enduring relationships with them.

Reading

Cochrane, Glynn. 1983. Policies for Strengthening Local Government in Developing Countries. Washington, D.C.: World Bank Staff Working Papers 582.

Eele, Graham, Joseph Semboja, Servacious Likwelile, and Stephen Ackroyd. 2000. Meeting International Poverty Targets in Tanzania. Development Policy Review 18(1):63–83.

Ferguson, James. 1994. The Anti-Politics Machine: "Development," Depoliticization, and Bureaucratic Power in Lesotho. Minneapolis: University of Minnesota Press.

Hicks, Ursula. 1960. Development from Below. Oxford: Clarendon Press.

Howard, Mary, and Ann V. Millard. 1997. Hunger and Shame: Child Malnutrition and Poverty on Mount Kilimanjaro. New York: Routledge.

Mawhood, Peter, ed. 1993. The Search for Participation in Tanzania, in Local Government in the Third World. 2nd edition. Pretoria: Africa Institute.

O'Rourke, Peter J. 1998. Eat the Rich: A Treatise on Economics. London: Picador.

6

Worker Elephants in the Mining Industry

When Papua New Guinea was still an Australian territory in 1960, geologists found low-grade copper mineralization on Bougainville Island. Over the next few decades, the economic contribution that a large copper mine at Panguna made to the economy of Papua New Guinea was immense. It generated 40 to 50 percent of all the country's foreign exchange and supplied some 20 percent of internal revenue. By 1990, however, the massive mine was closed. A civil war on the island resulted in the loss of thousands of lives. Bougainville tried and failed to secede from Papua New Guinea. It is now an autonomous province.

In 1975, a few years after leaving the Solomon Islands, I went as a consultant on a World Bank mission to Papua New Guinea to assess that country's credit worthiness on the eve of independence. The mission had some concerns about the future of the great mining enclave on Bougainville Island. The island's ethnic and cultural ties were to the south with the Shortland Islands, Choiseul, and the Western District of the Solomon Islands. At that time, it was common knowledge both in the Solomon Islands and in Papua New Guinea that Bougainville wanted to secede from Papua New Guinea and join the British Solomon Islands. Toward the end of the World Bank mission, I was sent to Honiara, the capital city of the Solomon Islands, to ask what the administration there would do if Bougainville wanted to join the

British Solomon Islands Protectorate. "Not very interested" seemed to be the reply.

The people of Bougainville resented the development of the Panguna mine of which most of the profits went to a government they disliked. The introduction of workers from elsewhere in Papua New Guinea was another problem and a primary reason for the closure of the mine and the ultimate break between Bougainville and Port Moresby, the capital of Papua New Guinea. Thousands of laborers had been brought in from the New Guinea highlands. The Bougainville people called them "redskins" because they were much lighter in skin color than the people in Bougainville. The highlanders' behavior was aggressive. They pushed and shoved and organized as a group to get their own way. When they didn't get their own way, fighting broke out. The "redskins" killed Islanders and raped Islander women. Bad feelings were exacerbated in 1982 when two prominent Bougainvilleans were killed in the New Guinea highlands after their car struck a young girl. The Bougainvilleans took violent action to expel all "redskins" from their island, and Panguna mine was closed in 1989.

Why Improve Community Relations?: The Bougainville Case

Rio Tinto's loss of its large copper mine at Panguna on Bougainville Island provided the company and others in extractive industry with a loud wake-up call. The period of civil unrest and violence in Bougainville, which extended from the 1970s to the 1980s, underlined the fact that international business, especially when working in developing countries, should have thorough knowledge of the social and political risks associated with large investments. It pointed out how important it is for companies to make sure that they understand sensitive social and political situations, and that they do nothing to exacerbate any existing tensions. It also indicated that international business involved in mining and other extractive industries needed to do more to protect and promote the welfare of affected communities.

The case of Bougainville did not seem to be so far away when, in 1995, Rio Tinto acquired an interest in the large mine that Freeport McMoran had in West Papua, Indonesia. Civil society organizations made accusations about human rights violations with some regularity. They said that Freeport employees put local people in containers, beat them, tortured them, and shot them. Subsequently, the Red Cross, the Catholic Bishops of Papua, and three other organizations conducted reviews and found no evidence that the company had been complicit in human rights violations. A lawyer who had been involved with human rights work at the International Court of Justice in the Hague, and who was also a board member of Freeport McMoran, conducted several investigations but found no evidence to support the allegations against the company.

Some of the accusations suggested a connection between the Indonesian Army and the company. It was frequently necessary to explain to civil society organizations from Australia and the UK that, in Indonesia, a foreign company's relationships with the army are prescribed by the Contract of Work agreement that forms the legal contract between the company and the government. Companies are required to cooperate with the army when requested.

In 1995, Sir Robert Wilson, the Chief Executive of Rio Tinto, one of the largest mining companies in the world, asked me to work for his company to improve its community relations. The term *community relations* encompasses a wide range of activities geared to improving the company's work and profit levels through informed and responsible relationships with people living in areas affected by the mines. At the time, Rio Tinto employed two hundred people in the corporate office in London and forty thousand people working at sixty overseas operations. Its mining operations were located in highly diverse environments and cultures, from the Mojave Desert in California, to the Atacama Desert in Chile, and the Carstensz Mountains of New Guinea.

In 1996, just after my first visit to the Freeport mine, the World Development Movement accused Freeport and Rio Tinto of causing the death by copper poisoning of over two hundred and sixty people at the Freeport mine in West Papua. Enquiries at the London School of Tropical Medicine and Hygiene revealed that death by copper poisoning of the sort suggested was unknown. Although this discrepancy was brought to the attention of the World Development Movement, the charge remained in a prominent place on their website for over a year.

In the 1990s, it was clear that the public had new expectations regarding the conduct of miners. The new guidelines established that if miners made a mistake—and they did make many mistakes, some of them very bad—the company had to acknowledge responsibility and try to fix the problem. The public expected that companies should not try to fix the problem with a public relations spin nor should they produce glossy brochures with pictures of happy, smiling local people. Dealing with social issues was like a professional golf game; you could not mark your own scorecard, others would do that.

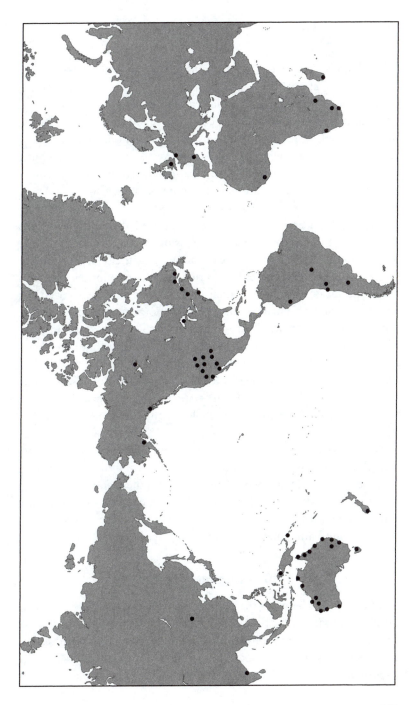

Rio Tinto's experience since the mid-1990s shows that attention to community relationships is as important to business success as the management of the plant or the minerals in the ground. Good community relationships reduced heavy costs in regulatory approval times, and prevented or reduced problems in construction, financing, and insurance, as well as helped to maintain investor confidence. If a mine had bad community relationships, local people would not be willing to be involved with it. International opinion was also increasingly important. Organizations of indigenous and other local people were gaining strength and visibility. They expressed their deep concerns with some of the serious negative effects of resource extraction, dam construction, and other large-scale projects in their territories. Rio Tinto was aware that the public in rich and poor countries alike had new expectations of international corporations that recognized the importance of defining and maintaining corporate social performance. If it was possible for Rio Tinto to find ways to help the poor in areas where it was involved, then it wanted to learn how to do so intelligently. The rationale for helping communities, however, was tied to the corporation's bottom line. If Rio Tinto was not commercially successful, then its ability to help the poor would disappear. Rio Tinto was also accountable to its shareholders and could not be reckless with their money.

When I came to Rio Tinto, I found that its employees were concerned that the risks of mining to the environment and to local people be understood and managed. Mining provides the metals that support everything in modern life, from computers to paint. Mining may also cause environmental and social changes that can be seriously damaging unless mitigating measures are put in place.

The Mining Process

The first contact between the mining business and local people occurs during exploration, the process of trying to find a commercially viable ore body. Most mining companies today try to ensure that their exploration staff is sensitive to social and cultural heritage issues as well as environmental risks. This was not so true in the past. Exploration can last for many years, and only one in a hundred exploration projects will produce a mine. In the exploration stage, geologists are the main characters who spend time in the local areas. Geologists sometimes live in close contact with communities for several years. They have to be aware of the consequences of their work, its impact on land or on sacred sites, as well as on local employment.

Exploration by mining companies requires a license from the host country government. Countries generate revenue by leasing out large tracts of land, often without the knowledge or consent of the citizens who live there. Some countries are more open to mining exploration than others. Critics of Rio Tinto have said that it owned half the ground in Norway. What Rio Tinto owned was a license to explore. While exploration licenses may cover very large areas, the actual mining footprint is much smaller. For example, the amount of ground used by Rio Tinto in 2007 in its many mines in Australia covers a smaller area than all the pubs in the country. Incidentally, Rio Tinto, in common with other companies, now provides funds directly to communities that they can use to pay for specialist advice when considering a new mining venture.

The second stage of the mining process is construction, which can last for several years. It produces particular social problems mainly related to the influx of large numbers of outsiders. Thousands of single men may descend on a remote location. Local people, instead of continuing their relationships with geologists they got to know in the exploration stage, now have to reckon with a totally different, and much larger, cast of characters. The construction workers' requirements for food and shelter place huge resource demands on the area and tend to result in dramatic price rises. The amount of cash in the local economy jumps exponentially. In order to support the mining operation, roads, ports, and even an airport are constructed. Many construction workers have sexual relationships with local women, and prostitution often flourishes where it had not existed before. Local people have to figure out how to make sense of and cope with all these dramatic and sudden changes in their physical and social environment. When the mine becomes operational, new problems arise. They range from recruitment of local people in the workforce to the plant's noise, the dust it creates, and other environmental effects.

A mine can often operate for 50 to 100 years. At some point, when the mine becomes unprofitable, management will decide to close it down. In earlier decades, mining companies proceeded with closure with no attention to social responsibility to the local people and the environment. By 1995, closure of a mine involved many complex challenges. The importance of environmental restoration and cleanup is assumed, and fairly clear guidelines, provided by the government and the company, exist on how to proceed. The best environmental restoration, through bulldozing and replanting, can leave a site with little evidence that a mine was once there.

Since mining can cause various kinds of damage it is important that the risks are clearly identified and that the best research is used to mitigate and contain damage. The environmental issues associated with mining are sometimes quite limited as was the case with ilmenite mined from mineral sands. The metal was captured by a mining process that worked its way along sand dunes. When mining was over, top soil and seed were provided, tree cover planted, and vegetation restored. In the Richards Bay area of South Africa where ilmenite mining had taken place, it was almost impossible to see where mining had been carried out. Copper mining sometimes had limited consequences as was the case with the very large Escondida mine in Chile. There all waste material, called tailings, was stored in the desert where, due to an absence of water there was little danger to the environment.

The giant Freeport mine in West Papua, Indonesia, was a different matter. Each day the mine discharged a quarter of a million tons of tailings into the river system with the result that a large area of the lowlands resembled the landscape of the Somme after World War I. Some suggested that the tailings could be piped down to the coast. However, this was not feasible because the area was exposed to high levels of seismic activity and if the pipe ruptured then there really would be a mess. Agronomists working in the tailings deposition area in the lowlands discovered that it was possible to re-vegetate these areas and to make gardens. As time went by, it appeared possible that the area could be turned into productive land. With the help of eth-nobotanists, trials were mounted to see if the types of banana and tuber popular among local people could be grown. As of 2007, these efforts continue.

At the end of mining, the pit that had produced the minerals had to be filled in and the lakes and ponds that had been used in the process-ing of the minerals had to be rendered safe. Filling in a mine pit can take a long time. One pit at a mine in South Carolina took ten years to fill. The physical task of closing would be complicated by several fac-tors that were hard to anticipate. Because it seemed a waste to disman-tle the buildings, local people tried to see if the buildings could be turned into a school or a government facility. In one instance a local government official said the buildings could be turned into a university campus. All structures had to be made earthquake-proof and arrange-ments had to be made to monitor the integrity of these structures for several decades or even a century.

It wasn't easy for journalist Agus Murdani, who was from Jogjakarta, to understand the world of the miner. These were people whose lives incline them to see things in black and white. They have a low tolerance for ambiguity. That makes it difficult for them to deal with social issues, where precision was hard to find.

On previous assignments he hadn't really come to grips with what a big mining company was like. The size of the equipment was amazing. Trucks so large that the driver could not see a car in front of him. That was why all the cars and jeeps had long aerials with flags on top. Millions of gallons of fuel were trucked to the site. They used enough explosives to start a small war. Power plants were constructed that could supply enough electricity to light a small city. Surveyors were everywhere, checking to see that their blueprint would become a reality. They moved mountains, filled valleys, diverted rivers, and obviously made a decent living.

Within the mining industry, there was debate about what should happen to the local people affected by closure. Typical skills of miners that had to do with moving earth were of no use here. Local people whose jobs depended on the mine faced immediate unemployment. They had become dependent on the mine-driven cash economy. Some ideas for dealing with this problem were to provide a large sum of money to each miner as compensation for loss of unemployment. Others reasoned that monetary compensation was not required because the local people had acquired transferable skills and knowledge as a result of mining. In their view, the best thing to do would be to help them put these assets to work elsewhere in the economy, an idea which did work. A few years after closure of one mine, another mining company arrived to find all the former employees had jobs and had ceased working in the mining industry.

Worker Elephants in Rio Tinto

Rio Tinto's community relations reminded me of my time in the Solomon Islands. I could see that the community relations practitioners that Rio Tinto had in the field were hands-on people with the skills and experience that came from spending many years in one region in contact with local people. They were also aware of global issues.

Miners have a sense of humor that can be disconcerting. I paid a visit to a mining exploration camp in the Lao People's Democratic Republic near the Ho Chi Minh trail in order to see the unexploded ordinance protection system that Rio Tinto was installing. The company wanted to protect local people living near the camp from little plastic fragmentation bombs that had been jettisoned by U.S. planes during the Vietnam War. Local people's living was based on a system of horticulture, in which they work a plot of land and then periodically abandon it to let it lie fallow and then clear a new plot. As they opened up new gardens, they encountered the unexploded bombs, and many adults and children had lost limbs as a result.

A geologist companion and I stopped by the local headman's house to pay our respects. As we were quaffing a clear and incredibly powerful local brew at the village headman's insistence, I noticed papaya seeds in the bottom of my glass. Nibbling on the seeds, I mentioned to my companion, a geologist, how odd it was that the British never ate papaya seeds whereas in Brazil, and now here in Laos, people did. Having looked carefully at the seeds, he said that he didn't doubt that papaya seeds were good for you but what was in the bottom of my glass was rat shit.

In my role as Community Relations Advisor, I helped develop a strong policy for improved social responsibility in the company and a team of socially trained local community relations practitioners. During my twelve plus years with Rio Tinto, it was refreshing to be back in the company of Worker Elephants after so many years of being surrounded by the other kind of elephant. I learned much about mining and about making it more accountable and helpful to local people.

Compared to how things were mishandled in Bougainville, the mining industry has come a long way in terms of paying attention to doing better by local people and the environment. A key to whatever success we had was strong and consistent support from the very top of the company. Rio Tinto sent clear messages that it was serious about improvement, and provided easy access to top managers without having to go through layers of bureaucracy. Another key factor was being able to build an excellent team of community relations specialists at headquarters and generalists at operations.

Although Rio Tinto had established good community relations at many of its operations, the goal in 1995 was to begin to bring all of the operations up to the best standard. Colleagues from mine sites all over the world and I launched the community relations improvement exercise by organizing a survey to get advice on improvement. This survey covered all of Rio Tinto's operations. The results reinforced the need for a *community relations policy* for the whole Rio Tinto Group. Headquarters developed this policy with the help of all operations. The policy stressed that, as with all social relationships, there was no guarantee of a particular result. Most important was the ongoing process of building and maintaining mutual understanding and respect between miners and local people.

As the volume of work increased and we gained more experience about the type of advice that operations found most helpful, the community relations team was expanded. The building of a good team and a worldwide network of practitioners required balance between geographical and functional coverage as well as balance between global and local skills. Headquarters staff—those with a doctorate or a master's degree—was recruited to provide specialized expertise of two kinds. Geographical expertise was acquired by practitioners who had lived and worked for ten to fifteen years in South America, Africa, Asia, and Europe. There was also a requirement for functional expertise in such areas as small business and supply-chain development, community health, education, and agriculture.

Five social scientists—three anthropologists, an archaeologist, and a small business expert—were hired to work as specialists at corporate headquarters in London and Melbourne, and to travel to operations providing advice and support. They all had substantial field experience in both the public and private sectors in both rich and poor countries. As advisors, it was not their job to drive the policy or to issue orders and instructions. The implementation of the communities' policy at a mine site was the responsibility of the managers who ran the mine. Visits by advisors to overseas operations were demand-driven. If the business did not ask for a visit, then a visit did not take place. It was the responsibility of advisors to keep abreast of the latest developments both inside and outside the industry, and to pass along information that might be of use to an operation.

Most of the community relations practitioners at operations were former geologists, engineers, teachers, or nurses who discovered that they had a talent for this kind of work. That makes sense. When someone has done the hard work of learning the local language and has made friends with local people, they are well on the way to being a community relations practitioner. They also had to get to know and understand the many kinds of people who work in the mining industry who I refer to in this chapter simply as "miners."

What Rio Tinto wanted was to build a two-way exchange between miners and local people. These relationships required realistic expectations on both sides. Experience had shown that it was always easier to raise expectations than to provide the means of their satisfaction.

Practitioners were expected to work with local communities, as well as with regional and national governments and other affected parties to reach agreed objectives. They were to plan on the basis of an expectation that social and economic progress required a long-term commitment from the miners and their neighbors if well-being was to be safeguarded and, where possible, enhanced throughout the life of a mine and beyond.

In designing these initiatives, Rio Tinto headquarters had to decide whether to award primacy to local culture over the potential importance of such global ideas as the Universal Declaration of Human Rights. Clearly, universal issues, such as possibly universal human rights, must be understood in terms of what they mean in local contexts. Most people now live in a situation where they are exposed to and move between universal ideas of justice and local interpretations and constructions of the same issues. UN approaches to the status and rights of women, for example, are universal, but rather than assuming such global principles can or ought to be universally applied, it makes sense to see how they fit or do not fit into particular local contexts and how local people may attempt to adopt and remake universal principles to suit their aspirations and constraints.

What mutual respect meant to a managing director might not be the same thing that it meant to someone at the bottom of the company. Headquarters personnel spent two years rolling out the policy at regional meetings round the world to ensure understanding of and buying in to the thinking and the objectives. Little would have been achieved if top management in London had not made it clear that advancement within the company would, in future, be dependent on doing a good job with social and community issues.

To ensure that operations realized the importance of the initiative to improve community relations, headquarters introduced a system requiring every overseas operation to produce a five-year plan, annually updated, to show what community relations meant for the business, the challenges, and the way the operation was complying with the community's policy. In the next five years, local operations produced over 300 plans. Specialist community practitioners in London then reviewed the plans and sent written comments to the operation. The plan would be discussed by the next corporate visitor to tour the operation. This process had a useful impact on the whole community-relations process, from exploration through to closure. It introduced a systematic way of approaching social issues.

Rio Tinto's Three-Step Communities Policy

Three basic steps involving specialist and generalist community practitioners were developed to implement the Communities Policy. The first step is the construction of a baseline to provide social information on the company's "neighbors" (the company's somewhat euphemistic term for people living in the areas affected by a mining project). The second step is establishing social relations with neighbors. The third step is attending to mutual aid or programs intended to help both the local community and the operation.

Step 1 Baseline Studies

Because mining kicked off and accelerated the speed of social change in the affected locality, it is critical to conduct baseline studies in order to later identify such changes, positive or negative. The baseline data help the company distinguish between changes that would have happened regardless of the presence or absence of the business and those caused by the business, directly or indirectly.

Baseline data can also identify trends in regional or local populations that might have an effect, over time, on the business. Such information might identify, for example, population increases that could not be sustained by existing government service provisions. For example, our baseline team in one part of West Papua in Indonesia discovered that people practiced "dry sex." This was the first finding of the practice other than in some parts of Africa. In "dry sex," a woman uses various methods to dry vaginal secretions before sexual intercourse in order to increase the pleasure of the man. It also may increase the possibility of vaginal lesions and HIV/AIDS transmission. This finding has relevance to the long-term health of local people involved in mining work. We brought it to the attention of other companies with large labor encampments that might attract prostitution.

Details of land use, land access, and land ownership arrangements were collected, as was information on ethnicity, social organization and leadership arrangements, health, food security, and education. Social maps showed the distribution of distinct ethnic groups, household sites, schools, churches, the town hall, gardens, grazing areas, forest plots, water wells, and who had rights to what. The baseline data were to be supplemented by existing or commissioned socioeconomic studies and ethnographic studies.

A baseline was expected to establish which neighbors were entitled to make a decision about a mining project. Some communities relied on decisions made by hereditary leaders; others had no well-defined leadership structures. As a result, a decision might be a long way from Western ideals of equal rights, since women's opinions, for example, might not be counted. Second, a baseline had to establish how what was proposed would be explained to local people who might be illiterate or not have radios. For example, in Madagascar, we employed artists to draw the proposed development. How will people make their opinions known? There might be no village hall. Villagers might be in their gardens all day or away fishing or hunting. It could be viewed as impolite for low status people to talk until their betters had made their opinions known. It might also be impolite for them to be in the same room as senior people. Ballot boxes? Local people might not be able to read or write. How should decisions be explained so that there was understanding and choice? Outsiders might not be able to understand the local language. How long should it take to reach a decision? Some decisions might have to be made over several weeks.

It was also necessary to try to ensure that neighbors had accurate information about the mining company. Community relations were not just about "us" understanding "them." "They" also had to understand miners. Local people needed to know what sort of people worked in the plant, what they did in the plant, and why they did what they did; for this reason, regular personal contact between neighbors and mine staff was essential. Companies had to ensure that they had people in regular contact with the community over a number of years. Most companies hold "open days," when local community members come to see what miners do. In the U.S., there was a tradition of hosting school and university students to see the scientific side of mining. Quite a few operations, such as US Borax, which has a visitor's center in the Mojave Desert in California, have museums to show the relationship between mining and its neighbors over the life of the mine.

Yolanda Bintulu was born in Samarinda, Indonesia, and had earned a doctorate at the University of California at Berkeley. As a government environmental manager working in Sulawesi, she was trying to learn if the illegal miners operating in the area were using mercury. These miners would pan for gold, scooping up gravel from the bottom of a river and swirling it around in a metal pan that had the same shape as a wok until small specks of gold that were heavier than the gravel settled at the bottom. By using mercury they could process much larger amounts of material. The mercury did not only make people's teeth fall out, it also would poison the river and kill its fish.

If they were using mercury, then the government would get blamed and would probably also have to close down legal smallscale mining in the area even though it had a spotless environmental record.

Yolanda began by talking with dentists because she knew that exposure to mercury causes people's teeth to fall out. She didn't find any evidence of people losing their teeth at abnormal rates.

Undertaking an ethnographic survey, or baseline survey, to see how local people made decisions, assumed considerable importance for Rio Tinto in the Mindinao area, in the southern Philippines. It showed that the critics who wanted to oppose exploration had not done their homework and did not speak for all the people in the exploration area. Columban order Roman Catholic missionaries protested the idea that Rio Tinto should explore for gold. I wondered how the missionaries had discovered the wishes of the Subanun people since over half of the Subanun were not members of the bishop's congregation. After all, Subanun (the name means "upland people" in much the same way that Montagnyard is used in parts of mainland Southeast Asia) had several widely dispersed bilateral kindreds (kinship groups that reckon kinship from both the maternal and paternal lines equally). They lived in isolated villages and had no form of fixed or hereditary leadership. How had the missionaries managed to get a definitive opinion from over a quarter of a million people living in this dispersed manner? Did the missionaries have data on how Subanun made decisions about something like exploration related to mining? To me, it seemed reasonable to have the missionaries' assertions checked by anthropological fieldwork. I located an anthropologist who had over thirty years of field experience in the area. I asked if he could find out who was speaking for whom. Many of the petitions against exploration that were sent to Rio Tinto had obviously been signed by only one person. Few of the Subanun were literate. Following the receipt of the anthropologist's advice that there were a number of viewpoints among the Subanun (with some for and some against exploration), Rio Tinto decided to cease all exploration in the Philippines.

A baseline study could also identify important aspects of the relationship between local people and their environment. Before my full-time involvement with Rio Tinto, I went to Panama in 1979 to undertake a baseline study so as to be able to later assess the possible effects of a copper mine on the indigenous Guaymi Indians. I discovered that, when the Spanish arrived, the Guaymi were forced to move off the flat part of the isthmus into the hills. As the Guaymi population expanded, they cleared more and more land, using the trees for firewood and construction. They had to move higher and higher into the mountains because of pressure from ranchers and because of their removal of tree cover. They subsequently lived on the continental divide between the Pacific and Atlantic Oceans in very cleverly constructed houses which protected their inhabitants from the high winds experienced in that region. When Spanish ranchers introduced cattle, the Guaymi lost their ability to maintain the crucial fallow cycle, which allowed their land to replenish itself. The combination of cattle herds, intensive cultivation, population increase, and the removal of trees and shrubs turned the land into concrete. The rains could not penetrate the soil but simply ran off the mountains. It was plain to see that the completed formal baseline would show that the Guaymi way of life was no longer sustainable. This fact had nothing to do with the presence or absence of a mine, but it was important because critics of the mining industry were saying that it was mining that was going to dramatically change the life of the Guaymi.

Critics of the Cerro Colorado project, who had not visited the Guaymi, saw mining as the inevitable destroyer of the unique and irreplaceable way of life of these indigenous people. Critics talked about the impact of industrialization on indigenous life as if they were dealing with a watch: remove one cog and the watch would not work. They envisaged a whole suite of disasters because they assumed that industrial development would change land tenure, cause resettlement, alcoholism, domestic violence, and a weakening of the authority of traditional leaders. Their *obiter dicta* might have carried more weight if they had undertaken fieldwork.

Soon after I joined the mining industry, I found that mountains in any land occupied by any indigenous people that miners might have an interest in were sacred. While I had no doubt that much land was sacred, it was also clear that civil society organizations strategically equated sacred mountains with indigenous people. I thought it might make for a restful change if we could have a sacred grotto. Within a short while I had my wish. As I approached a sacred spring, while I was on a "due diligence" survey of a property owned by another company (to see if the property represented value for money and was in compliance with current laws and regulations), a jet of water that would have done credit to the fountain on Lake Geneva suddenly shot out of the small, but reverently tended, grassy hollow. I asked the engineer who was my guide, if this sort of water pressure had always been present. "Well," he said, "we were worried that dewatering (a mining term) in the pit might have stuffed the water table so we decided to pump in some water. Pretty good now isn't it?" Fortunately, local people had no problem with the new fountain.

Any resettlement project needs a baseline to show conditions before and after any move, as well as whether those people affected have been able to choose to go or to stay. A Zimbabwean company in which Rio Tinto had a controlling interest had been exploring for diamonds several hundred miles from Harare and had found a small deposit. As part of the development of the diamond mine, Rio Tinto agreed to design a resettlement plan for several hundred people who were living close to the proposed mine site. The land was of poor quality. The people were suffering from food shortages and had been assisted by CARE. In fact, they were already in line for a government resettlement scheme. Rio Tinto's local advisors visited the people to explain how resettlement in other parts of the Rio Tinto group had been handled and to explain the latest international thinking on resettlement standards. As opposed to the common assumption that all resettlement is "involuntary," in this instance, the people wanted to relocate and had been waiting for several years for government to give them land on which to settle. The resettlement would be planned and executed by Zimbabwean nationals from the company's community relations department. A strong Zimbabwean team of community relations personnel—both men and women—had been in close contact with the community throughout exploration and then during construction.

Four individuals, however, wanted to remain and their wish was accommodated. The settlers themselves decided to walk to the farms that had been purchased by the company, where they took possession of the plots that had been surveyed and marked off. The company had promised "like for like" replacement, with the exception that the quality of the land in the new location was better. Each settler household head was given a house, water tank, cattle pens, and a water storage tank. His or her eight hectares of land were cleared of trees and ploughed. Special arrangements were made for the old and infirm or families lacking an able-bodied male. Roads were built through the settlement, and a small school and health center were staffed and equipped by government. Community relations personnel and engineers visited each settler household and made a "snag" list of things that had not been done right or which still had to be done. When all the work was complete, the resettlers signed or made their mark to show that the company had kept its side of the bargain.

Community baselines for new mines must consider the possibility of a "honey pot effect"—economic migrants arriving at the site in order to find work. In the 1980s, the population of one Indonesian town near a mine was less than 1,000 people. As a result of an almost

20 percent growth rate, the population of the town grew in the 1990s to over 120,000. It attracted migrants from all over Indonesia. But, with a financially strapped government, the new town posed massive problems for the company. It had no fire service, no reticulated water supply, and no electricity-generating capacity—these things had to be supplied by the company.

Developers usually have to undertake an environmental and Social Impact Assessment (SIA) before they get permission to develop a large project. SIAs have proved to be useful in the U.S., where it was born in 1970 when the National Environmental Policy Act (NEPA) was signed into law by President Nixon. Section 102 of the Act required Federal agencies to make "integrated use of the natural and social sciences in decision-making which may have an impact on man's environment." SIAs did not require the "best" or the "right" decision. Nor was there a requirement to stop projects with negative consequences. The emphasis was on public disclosure.

Rio Tinto complies with whatever regulations are in place, and it goes beyond these requirements in order to meet the aspirations of the community's policy. The Rio Tinto baseline procedure and subsequent steps in the community's policy provide much more assurance that the wishes of local people will be understood and accommodated than would be the case if the company relied on conventional SIAs alone. There are no standards for SIAs. Some are short documents; others are very long and tedious. They are all about written reports and thus not always helpful to communities where rates of literacy are low. SIAs are too often all about harm without pointing to the positive developments that must be part of any large modern industrial development. The words "mitigate and compensate" are the most commonly used terms in SIAs. In other words, you can hear the car hit the body—not a very even-handed approach to assessment of proposals that will cause positive as well as negative social change.

SIAs in developing countries often rely on the opinion of a single social scientist who may not know the community, the language, who to talk to, or who the community leaders really are. Social impact analysis in the U.S. addresses the "unintended consequences" of developments that are normally initiated by private, profit-oriented, companies. It is very hard for an analyst on a short visit to a community to work out what these "unintended consequences" might be. When Rio Tinto undertakes a baseline, a multidisciplinary team will be used, there will be extensive discussion with the local community, and local views will be prominent—as well as the way neighbors weigh the good and the bad points about the development. Those who take part in the baseline exercise will continue to have relationships with the involved community. SIAs in the U.S. have also given priority to local opinions because the opinion of groups of experts has been shown to be no better than local opinion. By contrast in developing countries, not only does a single analyst often conduct an SIA, but that analyst may be ignorant of the mining industry. They may, without challenge, be allowed to act on a personal belief in the need to avoid change rather than the need to accommodate the sorts of change that communities want.

Step 2 Establishing Social Relationships

Helping a poor person out of poverty takes time and effort, and social involvement to understand the person's particular situation, needs, and aspirations. I was reminded of just how hard it is to help one disabled person during my involvement with the Iron Ore Company of Canada, which had its operations near Labrador City in Newfoundland. The miners wisely realized that they should think about trying to help a small number of poor people rather than assuming they could help thousands of people to escape from poverty. In 2001, the West Labrador Employment Corporation in Canada had a program to help poor individuals to get jobs in the mining industry. It wanted to design help that focused on the ability of poor people, rather than their disability.

Seven years after the Employment Corporation began work in the living room of one of the founding members, it had managed to place eight individuals with various emotional and physical disabilities in jobs in Iron Ore of Canada, a local company. Each disabled individual had to be carefully assessed by human relations personnel to see what potential he or she possessed. Then, working closely with the mining company, jobs had to be designed to fit that individual. Instead of having to carry the entire task of caring for their loved ones, families with disabled men and women were able to share the care with a business, and the individuals who were employed as a result of the scheme were delighted to earn money for the first time in their lives.

Building and maintaining community relations has to be done *with* neighbors rather than *to* neighbors. To be successful, relationships have to be face-to-face and animated by mutual understanding, trust, and respect. Community relations practitioners have to get along well with local people.

Good community-level implementation required people who wanted to be in touch with, and touched by, ordinary people in communities. Such people were usually nationals of the country where the mining operation was situated. We found that Indonesians worked best with Indonesians, Chileans with Chileans, and South Africans with South Africans, and so on. Most of our community relations practitioners also had gained some exposure to economics, agriculture, anthropology, and other disciplines and professions relevant to their work in the field.

Community relations are two-way relationships, with each party giving and receiving something of value. This was underlined by another experience I had in Brazil. In a town near a small gold mine in Paracatu, near Brasilia, the capital, unemployment reached 40 percent. At night, some of the unemployed invaded the plant looking for things to steal. They also stole the material from which gold had been extracted, in the hope that they could recover enough gold to make the work worthwhile. There was a constant danger of violence escalating as security guards clashed with the invaders. The number of night invasions was running at the rate of 11,000 a year, or 30 per night.

The mine manager went to the town and held several meetings with local people. He asked them to help think of ways to reduce the night invasions because he was worried about the violence. He pointed out some of the things the company was doing and asked, in return, for their help. Employment was a key issue for the local people. In response, the company worked with state organizations and other businesses to see what jobs the private sector could create in the town. The company built and ran a clinic, and also financed the manufacture, and distribution of free, generic medicines. Another program was started to show unemployed youths how to collect and turn plastic and organic rubbish into brooms and to recycle paper. Land was acquired to establish vegetable gardens and several thousand tons of food was being produced for sale by a cooperative that the company sponsored. The number of night invasions soon dropped to under eight a week.

Not all Brazilian initiatives ended on such a positive note. A well-organized community campaign tried to get Rio Tinto to finance the construction of a religious statue on a nearby hillside. Such a statue, inspired by the famous one at Rio de Janeiro, could help boost the fledgling tourist industry. Eventually, a senior figure in the company made a donation of 100 bags of cement in the hope that this would help the company's reputation. When Rio Tinto employees accompanied locals on a visit to the completed statue, which was visible for all to see in the town below, they had to agree that the statue certainly looked impressive and was well made. But they were puzzled as to why, instead of a likeness of Christ, the face on the statue was that of the mayor, who happened to be running for re-election.

Step 3 Partnership

In 2000, massive fires broke out in West Kalimantan, the Indonesian part of the island of Borneo, due to the combined role of illegal logging by large companies and the freak weather patterns of El Niño. Passengers on planes flying into the area could not see the ground because of the dense smoke, which, along with the overpowering smell of burning wood, greeted them on landing. Local townspeople wore face masks, and their eyes streamed with tears from painful contact with the smoke.

In response to the disaster, Kelian Equatorial Mining (KEM), a subsidiary company of Rio Tinto, began to import and distribute several thousand tons of food to avoid the threat of starvation. KEM was the relief operation on the ground that helped local communities cope with the situation, and it saved many lives. It was staffed by a number of Indonesian technical personnel with strong community skills. In addition to being native Bahasa speakers (the lingua franca of Indonesia), they had also learned various local languages. At the time when the drought struck, there was a shortage of suitable transport. Company helicopters were used, but delivery by air often proved difficult because of the smoke created by the forest fires.

Compared to KEM, the global aid agencies working in the area lacked the necessary local knowledge and language skills to assess need and to deliver relief. Typically, they would have hired consultants to come in, but famine prevention and relief could not be effectively carried out by flown-in consultants with no local knowledge. Program implementers had to know where and how to purchase food supplies, how long delivery would take, and how reliable the suppliers would be.

The fires had one bizarre and quite unanticipated result: Rats emerged as one of the winners in this disaster, because the snakes that had kept the rats in check in the forest were killed in the inferno. An expanding population of rats then began to attack the villagers' rice granaries. Within a short time the rats had destroyed some 50 to 60 percent of the rice. This, combined with the destruction of rice being grown, resulted in thousands of villagers facing starvation.

The KEM foundation had a professional agriculturalist that was able to undertake a number of agricultural surveys to assess local food security. Subsequent follow-up surveys showed that soil fertility had declined after the forest fires. In consultation with the villagers, KEM arranged to supply seed and fertilizer, and help plant sufficient vegetable crops to ensure that food security would not be an immediate worry.

Rio Tinto has undertaken community development projects in partnership with local communities, if the local people express willingness to help themselves, and if the company could avoid dependency. This work required active partnership based on trust, shared involvement, and joint commitment. Obviously, the case for this sort of involvement is compelling in remote operations in developing countries where government services are weak and a wide gap exists between people's aspirations and the means of their satisfaction. One lesson emerged quite clearly, everywhere: The corporation could not buy goodwill. It had to be earned. Members of low-income communities often want the help that mining companies can give them. Mining companies know that if their operation is to succeed, local people need to become participants in the operation, investing their time and energy to support the initiative. What the Rio Tinto approach seeks is an informed investment decision from local people who want to become active participants, rather than pursuing a social license to operate from passive spectators. The thinking in the mining industry has gone through several phases since the 1970s, from a paternalistic and do-good phase that treated local people as recipients of help, to a phase where companies form a genuine partnership with the local people with the objective that the people become participants in the business. In contrast to this approach, many private sector companies do what they call "social investment." I have always thought that the term "social investment" was a little presumptuous on the part of foreign companies. Surely their job should be to fit into the local social landscape rather than assuming they can stand out by improving local society? How would the companies or distant civil society organizations know what they could and could not improve for local people? Such distant organizations had about as much insight in this direction as the public sector Festival Elephants described earlier in this book.[1]

One of the earliest, culturally informed, and therefore successful approaches to partnership was the establishment of a foundation, Rio Tinto Zimbabwe. Its trust deed stipulated that the objective was to advance the welfare of local people. A company that had been operating in Zimbabwe since World War I started the foundation for socio-economic development into which one percent of pre-tax profits was paid. The foundation looked for areas where its funds could make the greatest impact. One example of the work of the foundation was the construction of an irrigation system for Rupiki in eastern Zimbabwe. This irrigation system, which is still in existence, helped farmers double and triple their annual cash incomes. Similar foundations were subsequently established by Rio Tinto in South Africa at the Palaborwa copper mine and at the Rossing uranium mine in Namibia.

These early foundations had the advantage that they were independent of mine management. This independence meant that they had flexibility in terms of designing projects. A disadvantage for the company, however, was that a foundation could get involved in activities far from the mine and thus not be in a position to help neighbors of the mine when situations of need arose. This happened in Namibia, where the Rossing Foundation was engaged in activities in the north of the country at a time when the town of Arandis, near Swakapmund near the border with South Africa, needed development assistance urgently. The town had been handed over to the local people but after a few years it became clear that they could not afford the upkeep of the infrastructure and the schools. The company had to return to try to help the town council raise more revenue and create more local jobs.

Community infrastructure, such as roads, buildings, common-use facilities, clinics, schools, and bore holes, can contribute significantly to improving the lives of members of mining-affected communities. Better roads, for example, can assist local commerce. In the north of Australia, a flying doctor service was supported in order to help improve healthcare for Aboriginal people living in remote areas. When the formal banking system could not cope with small loans at a South African mine, the company came up with the idea of establishing a pavement bank near their Richard's Bay mine to provide women with the money they needed to trade on a daily basis in the market. The premises consisted of a freight container that had been turned into two rooms. In the morning, funds, for which a service charge was levied, were handed out, and in the evening the money was repaid. Borrowers and lenders knew each other, the default rate was zero and, when a thief tried to steal from the till, women traders caught him and handed him over to the police. At a Rio Tinto operation in Vermont, a helicopter pad, constructed by an operation that produces talcum powder, aimed to assist with medical evacuation. Within a month of completion it had helped to save a life. Practitioners came up with solutions to fit local social circumstances, and they did so quickly and with a minimum of fuss. However, when they had a working solution they did not hawk it around the world to try to get all other operations to adopt it. Such programs provide tangible evidence of the benefits of the mine's presence.

Sometimes companies made substantial community donations. They decided (and each operation had to make its own decision that had to be endorsed by its shareholders) to build schools, hospitals, and sports facilities. Mining companies, unlike some of the global aid agencies discussed earlier in this book, did not aim to become a substitute for government. Under normal conditions, good governments are responsible for providing basic health, education, and infrastructure. However, in countries where governments lacked the necessary resources, where locally delivery was poor, or where basic services were nonexistent, there was often an expectation on the part of local people and local government that the business would pay for such services. Over time, host governments and local people began to regard these benefits as an enduring entitlement. Rio Tinto, while interested in mutual aid, had to try to avoid making the host country dependent on its funds for services that the country's government should provide.

Big business often hands over large sums of money to local communities for socioeconomic development and for compensation for land acquired for development, extraction such as mining, or as rental. In the case of funds provided for socioeconomic development, discussion sometimes considers whether the company should specify what the money should be used for or if nothing should be said even though it may be clear that the money may be wasted. When mining companies spend millions on community welfare they want to know that the money is well spent. On one occasion, however, a respected tribal leader in New Guinea said that outsiders should not tell them how to spend their money: "If it is my pig, I decide how to cut it up." One year the recipients built over 200 houses of the same design because a leader had a relative with a house plan on his computer. Another time, there was a preference for all-terrain vehicles. Learning how to spend money wisely takes time, especially for people who are new to the concept of money itself. Education, and the fact that local people are being trained as plumbers, carpenters, electricians, bricklayers, and managers should gradually increase the ability of people who are new to money to handle it more responsibly.

An alternative to simply handing over large sums of money is to design and structure contributions from the business to the community as if the business were an aid agency. In developing countries, some businesses have developed a range of activities that were similar to those of bilateral or multilateral development agencies. They addressed weak service delivery, agriculture, education, enterprise development, and so on. The approach did not rely on the comparative advantage of the mine, or the skills of a large number of its employees to identify and manage activities. But funds were often wasted because operations did not have professional agriculturalists or education specialists.

Many Rio Tinto operations (as of 2007) favor a business approach when making a contribution from the company to local community welfare. This approach assumes that the business itself, and the skills of its employees, should be used to promote community development and welfare. It relies on things miners know how to do, such as technical training or helping small businesses supply goods and services. Jobs and training, contracting, and supplying have become issues in which local communities have a strong interest.

The ability of a business operation to share its wealth with the host country or affected community members depends on many factors. First, it depends on the country concerned sending royalty and tax money back to regions where the minerals were mined. One problem in getting more money from mining to stay in remote areas is fact that the modern mining technology is capital intensive. In remote areas of poor countries, there is not much a company can buy, so purchases often have to be made offshore. Realizing this, most mines now begin to plan procurement so as to maximize the amount that they can spend locally. It may not be possible to source the large quantities of acid that processing may require, but it should be possible to source food for the canteen, cleaning services, and making uniforms. Assessment will also look carefully at employment to try to see how many local people can be hired, and if there are measures that could be taken such as extra training or the redesign of jobs that could increase the numbers.

Compare Rio Tinto procedures and their value for local communities to the idea that mining companies should simply get "free, prior, and informed consent" from members of local communities before they start a mine. How would "free, prior, and informed consent" be achieved without having good baseline data, solid social relationships, and a positive approach to partnership? Such consent cannot be given or received as a one-time exercise. The exercise has to be repeated throughout the life of a project.

Future Challenges

Recent experience in Indonesia, Madagascar, Guinea, Brazil, and Mongolia suggests that few companies will be able to handle the wide range of national, regional, and local challenges posed by megaprojects on their own. A megaproject is a a project with national, rather than local effects, which has the potential for generating large revenues and which is likely to involve coordination among the country government, global aid agencies, and civil society institutions. Megaprojects have the capacity to add 20 to 40 percent to a country's gross domestic product. They will thus change the industrial-skills landscape at national, regional, and local levels while providing the money to finance health and education programs.

Because megaprojects can raise mega-expectations, developers must try to ensure a quick production of benefits while working in partnership with governments that probably have weak implementation capacity. While seeking a quick production of benefits, it is necessary to avoid becoming a surrogate government by entering into open-ended financing of a whole series of social development programs for which donors (rather than mining companies) have the skills and the remit to implement.

Personnel who are familiar with the conduct of affairs in large, organized public and private institutions will assist with the development of an institutional development strategy encompassing government ministries and departments, civil society, and global aid organizations.

To form these coalitions, a champion is needed—someone with sufficient convening power to bring all the key players to the table and to keep them on task for the long period of time that planning and preparing these megaprojects requires. This is a role that is well suited to global aid agencies, but companies wishing to develop such an institutional arrangement must establish a partnership that produces more value for local communities than would be achieved if a company and aid agency acted alone. The synergies between aid and business should be exploited. Companies build roads, ports, power plants, and water supply facilities, and these can stretch aid dollars by providing agencies with electricity, clean water, and infrastructure. To be most successful, they must understand that public agencies and private sector firms have different priorities, decision-making processes, and deadlines which need mutual accommodation.

Companies and their neighbors must do all they can to provide imaginative training programs for local people so that they can get and retain good jobs. At the same time, efforts must be made to try to build the supply chain for the operation in order to ensure that as much wealth as possible stays in the local economy.

During the late 1990s and the following decade when we developed the Rio Tinto community relations policy, the personal support of both the chairman and CEO ensured that we were able to establish high standards of community relations. This leadership set a benchmark for community relations throughout the project cycle. The case for strong community relations is compelling, and several big companies are developing their capacity in this direction. Smaller companies are just waking up to the fact that they should do so. At the same time, state-owned companies in Asia and Africa tend to continue to operate at a low level of community relations.

More companies are beginning to realize the importance that social issues have at several stages in the project cycle, as well as the damage that can be caused to a company's reputation by poor performance. Senior executives need to have a personal sense of the quality of practitioner personnel, their breadth of experience, and the reliability of their judgment. There is no way this can happen in the absence of regular contact. If top executives do not want to leave their offices, if they think of themselves as too important to meet personally and regularly with community relations practitioners, or if they think that all they need to know will come in a report to them or to some board committee, then community relations will not thrive.

My experience indicates that it is helpful if the community relations function is relatively freestanding and self-contained—though having close connections with other important departments, such as human resources and health and safety. Many companies have joined their community relations function to their external relations department. While there is a case for this, caution is also necessary because companies with large media staff, and with a joint community relations and external affairs function can be tempted to subordinate community relations to media possibilities. If they do, they will then worry much more about getting in the good books of civil society than they do about getting in the good books of their neighbors. Also, companies should keep in mind that community relations has an important internal function, one that should involve top management receiving advice on the selection, training, and performance of the company's overseas personnel. This suggests the need for a close liaison with personnel or human resources departments.

Some companies believe that community relations should be tied to their environmental department. Community relations are less precise in its assessments than environmental science. Environmental science professionals in their offices at corporate headquarters can understand a great deal without visiting a site. They can work on water use and quality, land use and management, energy use, waste disposal, and so on, because measurements are available and these can be checked against local, national, and international standards. Environmentalists have to try to avoid strained relationships with local communities, for whom the quality of their habitat is a central concern, by paying attention to local perceptions about the environment and local knowledge about its management. At the same time, environmental professionals must pay attention to local perceptions of the environment and local knowledge about its management. In the case of an operation on Lihir, Papua New Guinea, local people thought that the mining process had caused the sea level to rise and turtles to vanish. It does not really help to deal with this claim by sweeping it aside as not "scientific." The rising sea argument is valid in terms of local beliefs, which, as their science, has just as much authority and persuasive weight for them as our own scientific thinking does for us.

Unless big mining companies continue to take community issues seriously, there will always be a Bougainville just around the corner.

To avoid this, global businesses will need to invest a great deal more in training and staff development for community relations practitioners. Of course, community relations may not be the only activity in need of more resources. Since the late 1990s, competition for resources within large companies has increased due to the challenges to improve safety and concerns about climate change, for example. Nevertheless, it seems reasonable to predict a bright future for community relations because of the growing recognition among business leaders that strong community relations can yield a competitive advantage and provide an assurance to shareholders and the public that a business is working in line with society's expectations.

1. Since the 1990s, the Corporate Social Responsibility (CSR) movement has been trying to measure and report on the responsiveness of big business to its social responsibilities. CSR is popular with civil society organizations because they feel that it can help to improve the sensitivity of business to the consequences of investment decisions. Three problems with the present approach arise, however, because its methods lack genuine attention to the "social." First, CSR tends to define "social" and, therefore "responsibility" as global rather than local. Second, no ground truthing local capacity has been built to provide assurance that assessments target local values, beliefs, and attitudes. Data collection and theorizing are more like Victorian armchair anthropology as described in Chapter 1. Third, CSR enthusiasts fail to understand that social relationships and social responsibilities are not mandated in some central place but are instead the outcome of local customs, traditions, and community voluntarism.

Reading

Ballard, Chris, and Glenn Banks. 2000. Resource Wars: The Anthropology of Mines. Annual Review of Anthropology 32:287–313.

Cochrane, Glynn. 1971. Development Anthropology. New York: Oxford University Press.

Connell, John, and Richard Hewitt, eds. 1991. Mining and Indigenous Peoples in Australasia. South Melbourne: Sydney University Press.

Gjording, C. 1981. The Cerro Colorado Copper Project and the Guaymi Indians of Panama. Cambridge, Massachusetts: Cultural Survival, Inc. Occasional Paper No 3.

Kirsch, Stuart. 2006. Reverse Anthropology: Indigenous Analysis of Social and Environmental Relations in New Guinea. Stanford: Stanford University Press.

Regan, Anthony J., and Helga M. Griffin, eds. 2005. Bougainville before the Conflict. Canberra: Pandanus Books, Research School of Pacific and Asian Studies, the Australian National University.

Rio Tinto. 2003. The Way We Work. London: Rio Tinto.

Wilson, Richard A., ed. 1997. Human Rights and Cultural Context: Anthropological Perspectives. London: Pluto Press.

The World Conservation Union. 2005. Report of the Roundtable on Mining and Indigenous Peoples Issues. Convened through the IUCN-ICMM Dialogue on Mining and Biodiversity. Gland, Switzerland: IUCN, November, 8–9.

7

⌇⌇

Reinventing
Worker Elephant Skills

Festival Elephants play a key role in global aid agencies whose job is ostensibly to end poverty. Yet poverty is thriving. And so are Festival Elephants. Many people in the agencies would sincerely like to help poor people, but they are constrained by their model of development. The agencies are well set up, well staffed, and well able to manage the global knowledge associated with big infrastructure projects such as roads, ports, financial systems, and urban development. But such projects do not address poverty directly. Agency staff who know how to design, implement, and manage these kinds of projects do not have the local knowledge and skills to handle the social and cultural factors involved in projects aimed to alleviate poverty directly as informed by a focus on the varied lives of the poor.

The challenge of integrating global knowledge and local knowledge is infinitely more difficult than infrastructural development. It demands not only establishing and maintaining social relationships between aid agency personnel and poor people but also a long-term local presence of the sort not envisioned by the agencies. As the Myth of Global Poverty, over time, has generated more and more money for the agencies, poor countries have become increasingly unable to ensure that the funds reach their poorest citizens. Big projects and programs tend to benefit the better-off people in poor countries. The negotiating and administration needed to move these large sums of money has required aid agency personnel to become increasingly removed from regular contact with poor people. When applied to poverty alleviation the agencies' development model, driven by the Myth, has resulted in ever-increasing amounts of money moved by ever-larger institutions whose staff possesses ever decreasing knowledge of the people they are meant to help.

There is considerable irony in the fact that some mining companies with global operations put more emphasis on cultural competence and local implementation skills than global aid agencies do. The message of this book is that global aid agencies need to abandon the Myth and adopt a different development model: one that integrates global and local knowledge and skills. The issue is not one of either developing global knowledge or skills or of developing local knowledge and skills but of developing mutually reinforcing sets of skills for global and local tasks. An aid agency that wants to be seen as a "Knowledge Organization" must also have local knowledge.

My sense is that if poverty is to be taken seriously then thousands of practitioners with the right skills will need to be placed at all levels of aid agencies, civil society organizations, and business organizations, from community relations work to policy-making. They will, in addition to global skills, need to have an aptitude for hands-on contact with poor people, an ability to work in institutional settings, foreign language skills, and cultural competence. At present, however, no system exists for the recruitment, training, and deployment of such professionals, though individual initiatives exist, such as those described for Rio Tinto in Chapter 6.

Paul Appleby, former Dean of the Maxwell Graduate School at Syracuse University, was asked by the Government of India to review their Civil Service just after Independence. He had some sound recruitment advice:

> The people who are broadly trained and practically oriented can learn the techniques more rapidly and better on the job. . . . it has a great bearing on the selection of students for professional training . . . . A university cannot confer outright all of the qualities implied . . . It can only add to the equipment of persons already strongly formed to the desired patterns. They should select not merely on the basis of strictly

academic account of skill in human relations, flexibility, diversified experience and varied acquaintance with people and activities of people. . . . They should select with the hope of finding persons peculiarly slanted toward the business of relating apparently unlike things, persons already in exceptional degree devoted to the public interest, and persons temperamentally bent toward action (1950).

The dedication and behavior of Worker Elephants cannot be programmed. Those who want to reinvent Worker Elephants must help build knowledge, skills, and values that will allow the organization to deal effectively with a variety of situations that cannot be predicted. Worker Elephants should be predisposed toward participative management—management that depends on everyone making a contribution rather than expecting everyone to follow what the boss dictates. They should have interpersonal skills, and at least a basic awareness and sympathy toward processes of collaboration. It would be destructive to recruit Worker Elephant candidates whose personal style relies on technique, dominance, authority, and enforcement. Too great a concern about management in the sense of routine, predictability, and perfection would not be desirable.

Developing motivation to learn is the most essential goal of any training program because practitioners will encounter novel situations that none of us can visualize in advance. What they need most is the incentive and the skills to learn about a unique situation and to invent a way to deal with it. Many Worker Elephants have substantial field experience, and as a result, see time as scarce and are less inclined to accept the assurance of their seniors about the inherent worth of a unit activity. They need to feel that value themselves. As a result, it is important to respect these dynamics in conceptualizing any development program.

Worker Elephants should be located in small and nimble organizations, either autonomous institutions or as a special unit within a larger institution. Any operation that proposes to train people to deal with poverty in a culturally informed and flexible way cannot be governed by established norms and must be free to move in uncharted directions. The need for freedom and opportunity to assume risk increases when the goals sought and the means of accomplishing them increase in ambiguity. For example, fairly specific norms of behavior and expectations can be applied to an engineering program; this kind of mission may need relatively little freedom. When the mission is to seek improvement in the condition of poor people around the world, on the other hand, the ambiguity is very high for two reasons: First, relatively little agreement exists about what should be done, about the necessary actions, or the required competence or experience. Second, we are not dealing with overt, predictable behavior.

The management climate must be one in which differences of approval are welcomed; mistakes are seen developmentally, rather than causes for punitive behaviour; risk takers are rewarded; and the leader's role is more one of supporter than of enforcer. The reverse point can be made that rules are not prized because they are not particularly functional in an organization that seeks to avoid predictability and conformity. It is apparent, of course, that operations do not fall easily into the polar positions of high predictability and conformity, and low predictability and nonconformity. They tend to be arranged on a continuum between the two extremes. Nevertheless, it is useful to recognize the extremes as a basis for understanding the kind of organization and climate that fosters innovation and improvement.

Worker Elephants should be discouraged from thinking of themselves as "donors" who supply all the bright ideas and resources required for success. They must understand that communities want to give as well as receive. In turn, they must understand that they are receiving something of value from their hosts. Generations of community practitioners—and I count myself as was one of them—know that they have benefited from living and working in other cultures, and they have brought those benefits back to enrich their own societies. As a result of their service, they grew to be better people than if they had stayed at home. By living overseas for some years, practitioners gradually come to understand that theirs is not the most important culture in the world—the one that less fortunate people do not possess. Instead, they learn to appreciate how other societies manage the business of living and dying and getting along, and how others have designed rituals and customs that show great delicacy and sensitivity.

If there were enough of us, we affected our host communities in some small ways that they thought to be useful.

It is equally important that Worker Elephants have a sound understanding of their own society and institutional functioning, as it is for them to become familiar with other cultures. Many people who work overseas do not know how and why the institutions and organizational forms in their homeland are the way they are, nor do they understand the forces that shaped them. They are familiar with institutions and organizational forms but not the *how* and the *why*. This knowledge of one's own society and cultural development is not merely a matter of knowing the history of your home country, it is also a matter of keeping current and up-to-date with what is happening in the present day. It is a matter of cultural competence.

When I first joined the British Overseas Civil Service in 1962, the British government, like many other colonial governments, realized the value of training its administrators in local cultures and languages. Our training inculcated a sense of service toward the people in the colonies, an interest in getting to know them, and a commitment to spending time with local people. Cultural anthropology (or social anthropology, as it is referred to in Great Britain) was a key component in training for the field. When I became an academic, I argued for the *anthropology of development*, a subfield of anthropology that includes in-depth training in cultural (social) anthropology combined with regional expertise, language study, economics, quantitative analysis coursework, and policy skills, with a hands-on, practical emphasis throughout.

Since then, many anthropology departments have moved toward postmodernist theorizing and away from practical application. Things may, I hope, change again to include the possibility of a more service-oriented, professional approach that would contribute to the growth and replenishment of skilled community relations workers. I do not support a return to colonialism or any notion that mining companies are completely benevolent entities uninterested in profit. Instead, my point is that there are lessons about poverty alleviation that can be learned from British colonialism and from mining. Perhaps this book will encourage others with different experiences in different countries and contexts to reflect on these experiences in terms of the negative effects of Festival Elephants and the Myth of Global Poverty. No matter how diverse our experiences, I think we can all agree that it is time to move on from these self-serving and ineffective approaches. Aid agencies used to provide real value and can do so again. What is needed is a cull of Festival Elephants, major downsizing and reorganization of staff, and a complete change of institutional culture in the global aid agencies and civil society organizations. These steps will make room for the right people with the right skills and attitudes, working in small numbers at headquarters and in large numbers in the field. It is high time to bring back the Worker Elephants.

Bibliography

Appleby, Paul. 1950. Address to the Institute of Public Administration of Canada, Toronto, September 20. Appleby Papers: Box 56. Syracuse University Archives, Syracuse, NY.

Ballard, Chris, and Glenn Banks. 2000. Resource Wars: The Anthropology of Mines. Annual Review of Anthropology 32:287–313.

Batten, T. R. 1957. Communities and Their Development. London: Athlone Press.

Baum, Warren, and Stokes Tolbert. 1985. Investing in Development: Lessons of World Bank Experience. Oxford: Oxford University Press for the World Bank.

The Bretton Woods Committee. 2004. Proceedings of the Meeting to Celebrate 60 Years for the World Bank and I.M.F. Washington, D.C., September.

Buck, Pearl S. 1984. Tell the People. Cavite: The Philippines, International Institute for Rural Reconstruction.

Cleveland, Harlan, and Gerard Mangone. 1957. The Art of Overseasmanship. Syracuse: Syracuse University Press.

Cochrane, Glynn. 1970a. The Administration of Wagina Resettlement Scheme (from the Phoenix group to Wagina, Manning St., Solomon Is. in 1964). Human Organization 29(2):123–32.

—. 1970b. Big Men and Cargo Cults. Oxford: The Clarendon Press.

—. 1971a. The Case for Fieldwork by Officials. Man 6(2): 279–84.

—. 1971b. Development Anthropology. New York: Oxford University Press.

—. 1974. What Can Anthropology Do for Development? Finance and Development 11(2):20–23.

—. 1979. The Cultural Appraisal of Development Projects. New York: Praeger.

—. 1983. Policies for Strengthening Local Government in Developing Countries. Washington D.C.: World Bank Staff Working Papers. No. 582.

Cochrane, Glynn, and Raymond Noronha. 1973. A Report with Recommendations on the Use of Anthropology in Project Operations of the World Bank Group. Washington, D.C.: The World Bank, Central Projects Division.

Connell, John, and Richard Hewitt, eds. 1991. Mining and Indigenous Peoples in Australasia. South Melbourne: Sydney University Press.

Crystal, David. 2000. Language Death. Cambridge: Cambridge University Press.

Dennis, Norman. 1998. The Invention of Permanent Poverty. London: Institute for Economic Affairs.

Denoon, Donald. 2000. Getting under the Skin: The Bougainville Copper Agreement and the Creation of the Panguna Mine. Melbourne: Melbourne University Press.

digim'Rina, Linus S. 2005. Food Security through Traditions: Replanting Trees and Wise Practices. People and Culture in Oceania 20:13–36.

Easterly, William. 2006. The White Man's Burden: Why the West's Efforts to Aid the Rest Have Done So Much Ill and So Little Good. New York: The Penguin Press.

Edwards, Michael. 2000. NGO Rights and Responsibilities: A New Deal for Global Governance. London: The Foreign Policy Centre.

Eele, Graham, Joseph Semboja, Servacious Likwelile, and Stephen Ackroyd. 2000. Meeting International Poverty Targets in Tanzania. Development Policy Review 18(1):63–83.

Elkington, John. 1997. Cannibals with Forks: The Triple Bottom Line of 21ˢᵗ Century Business. Oxford: Capston.

Elton, Geoffrey R. 1948. An Early Tudor Poor Law. Economic History Review 6(1):55–67.

Ferguson, James. 1994. The Anti-Politics Machine: "Development," Depoliticization, and Bureaucractic Power in Lesotho. Minneapolis: University of Minnesota Press.

—. 1998. Anthropology and its Evil Twin: Development in the Constitution of a Discipline. In International Development and the Social Sciences. Frederick Cooper and Randall Packard, eds. Pp. 150–175. Berkeley: University of California Press.

Firth, Raymond. 1963. We the Tikopia. Boston: Beacon Press.

—. 1964. The Elements of Social Organization. Boston: Beacon Press.

Foster, Robert. 2002. Materializing the Nation: Commodities, Consumption, and Media in Papua New Guinea. Bloomington: Indiana University Press.

Frank, Robert, Thomas Gilovich, and Dennis Regan. 1993. Does Studying Economics Inhibit Co-operation? Journal of Economic Perspectives 7(2):159–171.

Furse, Robert. 1962. Ancuparius: Memoirs of a Colonial Recruiting Officer. London: Routledge.

Galbraith, John Kenneth. 1979. The Nature of Mass Poverty. Cambridge: Harvard University Press.

Gill, William Wyatt. 1984. From Darkness to Light in Polynesia. Apia, Western Samoa: University of the South Pacific Commercial Printers.

Gjording, Chris. 1981. The Cerro Colorado Copper Project and the Guaymi Indians of Panama. Cambridge, Massachusetts: Cultural Survival, Inc. Occasional Paper No. 3.

Goodland, Robert. 1999. Social and Environmental Assessment to Promote Sustainability: An Informal View from the World Bank. Glasgow: International Association of Impact Assessment.

Hancock, Graham. 1989. The Lords of Poverty: The Power, Prestige, and Corruption of the International Aid Business. New York: Atlantic Monthly Press.

Hanlon, Joseph. 2004. Do Donors Promote Corruption? The Case of Mozambique.Third World Quarterly 25(4):747–763.

Hann, Chris, and Elizabeth Dunn, eds. 1996. Civil Society: Challenging Western Models. New York: Routledge.

Heap, Simon. 2000. NGOs Engaging with Business: A World of Difference and a Difference to the World. Oxford: The International Non-governmental Organisation Training and Research Centre.

Hicks, Ursula. 1960. Development from Below. Oxford: Clarendon Press.

Hill, J. F. R., and J. P. Moffett. 1955. Tanganyika, A Review of Its Resources and Their Development. Dar-es-Salaam: Government Printer.

Hobbs, Nathaniel. 2005. Corruption in World Bank Financed Projects: Why Bribery is a Tolerated Anathema. London: London School of Economics and Political Science, Development Studies Institute.

Hogbin, Ian. 1944. Native Councils and Native Courts in the Solomon Islands. Oceania 14(4):257–83.

—. 1958. Social Change. London: Watts.

Holme, Richard, and Phil Watts. 2000. Corporate Social Responsibility: Making Good Business Sense. London: World Business Council for Sustainable Development.

Hood, Christopher. 1990. Beyond the Public Bureaucracy State? Public Administration in the 1990s. Inaugural lecture, London School of Economics.

Howard, Mary, and Ann V. Millard. 1997. Hunger and Shame: Child Malnutrition and Poverty on Mount Kilimanjaro. New York: Routledge.

International Federation of Chemical, Energy, Mine, and General Workers Union 1997. Rio Tinto: Tainted Titan. Brussels: The Stakeholders Report.

IUCN [The World Conservation Union]. 2005. Report of the Roundtable on Mining and Indigenous Peoples Issues. Convened through the IUCN-ICMM Dialogue on Mining and Biodiversity. Gland, Switzerland. November 8–9.

Jenkins, Glenn P. 1994. Modernization of Tax Administrations: Revenue Boards and Privatization as Instruments for Change. Bulletin for International Fiscal Documentation 48(2). Amsterdam: IBFD Publications BV.

Khan, Mushtaq. 2002. Corruption and Governance in Early Capitalism: World Bank Strategies and their Limitations. In Reinventing the World Bank. J. Pincus and J. Winters, eds. Pp. 164–184. Ithaca, NY: Cornell University Press.

King, John A. 1967. Economic Development Projects and their Appraisal. Baltimore: Johns Hopkins University Press.

Kinuthia-Njenga, Cecilia. 1996. Civil Society: New Roles for African Traditions, NGO's, Women and Youth in Africa. Development 3:24–27.

Kirsch, Stuart. 2006. Reverse Anthropology: Indigenous Analysis of Social and Environmental Relations in New Guinea. Stanford: Stanford University Press.

Klitgaard, Robert. 1988. Controlling Corruption. Berkeley: University of California Press.

Liese, Bernhard H., Paramjit S. Sachdeva, and D. Glynn Cochrane. 1991. Organizing and Managing Tropical Disease Programs. World Bank Technical Paper 159. Washington, D.C.: The World Bank.

Little, Paul E. 2005. Demanding Accountability: Civil Society Claims and the World Bank Inspections Panel. American Anthropologist 107(3):514–515.

Mair, Lucy P. 1948. Australia in New Guinea. London: Christophers.

Mallaby, Sebastian. 2005. The World's Banker. New Haven, CT: Yale University Press.

Mammo, Tirfe. 1999. The Paradox of Africa's Poverty. Lawrenceville, NJ: The Redsea Press.

Marcus, George. 1995. Ethnography in/of the World System: The Emergence of Multi-Sited Ethnography. Annual Review of Anthropology 24: 95–117.

Masefield, Geoffrey B. 1950. A Short History of Agriculture in the British Colonies. Oxford: Oxford University Press.

Marshall, Dorothy. 1937. Revisions in Economic History VII: The Old Poor Law, 1662–1795. Economic History Review 8(1):38–47.

Matane, Paulias N. 1982. The 'Big-Man' Qualities of Effective Leadership in Traditional and Modern Societies. Administration for Development 18:26.

Mawhood, Philip. 1993. The Search for Participation in Tanzania. In Local Government in the Third World: The Experience of Decentralization in Tropical Africa. 2nd edition. Philip Mawhood, ed. Ch 4. Pretoria: Africa Institute of South Africa.

Mayfield, James B. 1986. Go to the People. West Hartford, CT: Kumarian Press.

McIntosh, Malcolm, Deborah Leipziger, Keith Jones, and Gill Coleman. 1998. Corporate Citizenship: Successful Strategies for Responsible Companies. London: Financial Times/Prentice Hall.

Meltzer, Allan H., et al. 2000. The Report of the International Financial Institution Advisory Commission of the United States Congress. Washington, D.C.

Meren, Michael. 1998. The Road to Hell: The Ravaging Effects of Foreign Aid and International Charity. New York: The Free Press.

Merry, Sally Engle. 2006. Human Rights and Gender Violence: Translating International Law into Local Justice. Chicago: University of Chicago Press.

Nunberg, Barbara. 1990. Public Sector Management Issues in Structural Adjustment Lending. Washington, D.C.: The World Bank.

O'Rourke, Peter J. 1998. Eat the Rich: A Treatise on Economics. London: Picador.

Paley, Julia. 2001. The Paradox of Participation: Civil Society and Democracy in Chile. Political and Legal Anthropology Review [PoLAR] 24(1):1–12.

Palmier, Leslie. 1985. The Control of Bureaucratic Corruption: Case Studies in Asia. New Delhi: Allied Publishers Private Limited.

Quodling, Paul. 1991. Bougainville: The Mine and the People. Pacific Papers 3. St. Leonard's, NSW, Australia: The Centre for Independent Studies.

Regan, Anthony J., and Helga M. Griffin, eds. 2005. Bougainville before the Conflict. Canberra: Pandanus Books, Research School of Pacific and Asian Studies, the Australian National University.

Rich, Bruce. 1998. Mortgaging the Earth: The World Bank, Environment and the Crisis of Development. Boston: Beacon Press.

Rio Tinto. 2003. The Way We Work: Our Statement of Business Practices. London: Rio Tinto.

Royal Dutch/Shell. 1998. Business and Human Rights: A Management Primer. London.

Sahlins, Marshall D. 1963. Poor Man, Rich Man, Chief: Political Types in Melanesia and Polynesia. Comparative Studies in Society and History 5:285–303.

Scope, Candid. 1976. Honest To My Country. Tabora, Tanzania: T.M.P. Book Department.

Scott, Dick. 1991. Years of the Pooh-Bah: A Cook Island History. Auckland: Hodder and Staughton.

Seebohm, Rowntree B., and G. Lavers. 1991. Poverty and the Welfare State: A Third Social Survey of Youth Dealing Only with Economic Questions. London: Longmans, Green and Company.

Short, Clare. 1997. Eliminating World Poverty: A Challenge for the 21st Century. Presented to Parliament by Command of Her Majesty, London, November.

Simmel, George. 1965. The Poor. Social Problems 13(2):118–140.

Smillie, Ian. 1995. The Alms Bazaar, Altruism under Fire: Non-profit Organizations and International Development. London: Intermediate Technology Publications.

Stern, Ernest. 1991. Beyond the Transition: 20th World Conference of the Society for International Development. Amsterdam.

Stocking, George W., Jr. 1996. After Tylor: British Social Anthropology 1888–1951. London: The Athlone Press.

Strathern, Andrew. 1982. Problems of Leadership and Communication in the Public Service in Papua New Guinea. Administration for Development 18:35.

Streeten, Paul et al. 1980. First Things First: Meeting Basic Human Needs in Developing Countries. New York: Oxford University Press.

Tolstoy, Count Leo. 1950. Anna Karenina. New York: The Modern Library.

Trollope, Anthony. 1992. An Autobiography. New York, Oxford University Press.

United Nations. 1996. Indicators of Sustainable Development: Framework and Methodologies. New York: United Nations.

—. Human Development Report (annual). New York: Oxford University Press.

Wade, Robert. 2005. International Organizations and the Theory of Organised Hypocrisy: The World Bank and Its Critics. Working paper. London: London School of Economics, Development Studies Institute.

White, Geoffrey M. 2003. Identity through History: Living Stories in a Solomon Island Society. New York: Cambridge University Press.

Wilson, A. Richard, ed. 1997. Human Rights and Cultural Context: Anthropological Perspectives. London: Pluto Press.

Wolfensohn, James D. 1999a. Address to the Board of Governors. Washington, D.C.: The World Bank. September 28.

—. 1999b. A Proposal for a Comprehensive Development Framework. Discussion Draft. Washington, D.C.: The World Bank.

The World Bank. World Development Report (annual). Washington, D.C.: The World Bank.

—. 1999. Poverty Trends and Voices of the Poor. Washington, D.C.: The World Bank.

Worsley, Peter. 1968. The Trumpet Shall Sound. New York: Schocken.

Wynn, Barry. 1966. The Man Who Refused to Die. London: The Souvenir Press.

Yekutiel, Perez. 1981. Lessons from the Big Eradication Campaigns. World Health Forum 2:465–490.

Yen, Yang-ch'u James. 1975. The Ting Hsien Experiment in 1934. Cavite, The Philippines: International Institute for Rural Reconstruction.

Young, Crawford. 1976. The Politics of Cultural Pluralism. Madison: University of Wisconsin Press.

Zadek, Simon. 2001. The Civil Corporation: The New Economy of Corporate Citizenship. London: Earthscan.